Title: Beyond the Horizon-The Ripple Revolution with XRP

Subtitle: Transforming the Financial Landscape

Series: Blockchain and Cryptocurrency Exposed

Author: Herman Strange

Table of Contents

Introduction

Definition of Ripple and XRP

Ripple is a real-time gross settlement system (RTGS), currency exchange, and remittance network that was created to transform how we move money around the world. Ripple was founded in 2012 by Chris Larsen and Jed McCaleb and is headquartered in San Francisco, California.

XRP is the native digital currency that runs on the Ripple network. XRP was created as a bridge currency to facilitate cross-border transactions and to help financial institutions move money faster and more efficiently. Unlike other cryptocurrencies like Bitcoin and Ethereum, XRP was not designed to be a store of value or to support smart contract technology.

The Ripple network and XRP are often used interchangeably, but they are two separate entities. The Ripple network is the underlying technology that powers the transfer of funds, while XRP is the digital asset that enables the transfer of value across the network.

Importance of Ripple and XRP in the Financial Industry

The traditional financial industry has been plagued by slow transaction times, high costs, and lack of transparency. Many of these issues can be traced back to the outdated legacy systems that banks and financial institutions still use today. Ripple and XRP have the potential to disrupt the traditional financial industry by providing a faster, more cost-effective, and more secure alternative to traditional cross-border payments.

The Ripple network's primary objective is to eliminate the inefficiencies of traditional banking systems by providing a decentralized, global, and real-time settlement infrastructure. The Ripple network allows banks and financial institutions to transact with each other directly, eliminating the need for intermediaries such as correspondent banks, which often lead to higher fees and longer processing times.

XRP, as the bridge currency of the Ripple network, helps financial institutions move money across borders more quickly and efficiently by eliminating the need for pre-funding and reducing foreign exchange costs. XRP transactions settle within seconds and have a fraction of the cost of traditional cross-border payments.

Overview of the Book and Its Purpose

The purpose of this book is to provide a comprehensive overview of Ripple and XRP, their history, technology, adoption, and potential impact on the financial industry. This book will explore the advantages of using Ripple and XRP in cross-border payments, the early adopters of Ripple and XRP, the regulatory landscape for Ripple and XRP, and the potential for Ripple and XRP to transform the financial landscape.

Through this book, we aim to educate and inform readers about the transformative potential of Ripple and XRP in the financial industry. We will explore the controversies surrounding Ripple and XRP, the criticisms of the technology, and the potential opportunities and challenges that Ripple and XRP face in the future.

By the end of this book, readers will have a comprehensive understanding of Ripple and XRP, their role in the financial industry, and their potential to revolutionize how we move money around the world.

Importance of Ripple and XRP in the financial industry

Ripple and XRP are becoming increasingly important in the financial industry. Their unique features and capabilities are transforming the way financial institutions, businesses, and consumers approach cross-border payments and currency exchange. In this section, we will discuss the importance of Ripple and XRP in the financial industry and their impact on traditional financial systems.

One of the main reasons why Ripple and XRP are important is their ability to offer fast, reliable, and cost-effective cross-border payments. The traditional international payment systems used by banks and financial institutions can be slow and expensive. It can take several days for a payment to reach its destination, and the fees can be high. Ripple and XRP aim to solve these problems by offering a decentralized, peer-to-peer payment system that is fast, secure, and cost-effective.

Another key feature of Ripple and XRP is their ability to provide liquidity for cross-border payments. Traditional payment systems often require banks and financial institutions to hold large amounts of different currencies to facilitate transactions. This can tie up valuable capital and increase the risk of currency fluctuations. Ripple and XRP solve this problem by providing a bridge currency that can be used to exchange different currencies quickly and easily. This can help reduce the amount of capital that banks and financial institutions need to hold and minimize the risk of currency fluctuations.

The adoption of Ripple and XRP by financial institutions and businesses is also important because it can help increase financial inclusion. Many people around the world do not have access to traditional banking services, and cross-border payments can be particularly difficult for them. Ripple and XRP offer a solution by providing a decentralized, borderless payment system that can be accessed by anyone with an internet connection. This can help increase financial inclusion and improve the lives of people around the world.

In addition, Ripple and XRP have the potential to transform the way money is moved around the world. The traditional financial system is often slow and cumbersome, and it can be difficult to track the movement of funds. Ripple and XRP offer a solution by providing a transparent, fast, and secure payment system that can be used to move money around the world quickly and easily. This can help reduce fraud, increase transparency, and improve the overall efficiency of the financial system.

Finally, Ripple and XRP are important because they are at the forefront of the blockchain revolution. Blockchain technology has the potential to transform many aspects of the financial industry, and Ripple and XRP are leading the way in this transformation. By using blockchain technology, Ripple and XRP offer a secure, decentralized, and transparent payment system that can be used to move money around the world quickly and easily.

In conclusion, Ripple and XRP are becoming increasingly important in the financial industry. Their unique features and capabilities are transforming the way financial institutions, businesses, and consumers approach cross-border payments and currency exchange. Ripple and XRP offer fast, reliable, and cost-effective cross-border payments, provide liquidity for cross-border payments, increase financial inclusion, transform the way money is moved around the world, and are at the forefront of the blockchain revolution.

Overview of the book and its purpose

The book "Beyond the Horizon - The Ripple Revolution with XRP: Transforming the Financial Landscape" is a comprehensive guide to the history, technology, adoption, potential, and criticisms of Ripple and XRP, two entities that have revolutionized the financial industry.

The purpose of this book is to provide readers with a thorough understanding of Ripple and XRP, their impact on the financial industry, and their potential for the future. By exploring the birth and evolution of Ripple and XRP, this book aims to offer a complete picture of the ecosystem and highlight its potential to transform the financial landscape.

Chapter 1 provides a detailed account of the creation of Ripple and XRP, the problem it aims to solve, and the technology behind it. Chapter 2 discusses the advantages of using XRP, its differences from Ripple, and the role of XRP as a bridge currency. Chapter 3 explores the adoption of Ripple and XRP, the benefits of using it for financial institutions, and the challenges in its adoption.

Chapter 4 delves into Ripple's role in the cryptocurrency market, compares XRP to other cryptocurrencies, and analyzes the impact of Ripple and XRP on the industry. Chapter 5 focuses on the Ripple community, its role in Ripple's success, and its impact on the ecosystem's development. Chapter 6 discusses the regulatory landscape for Ripple and XRP, the SEC lawsuit against Ripple and XRP, and its implications.

Chapter 7 explores the untapped potential of Ripple and XRP, its use cases beyond cross-border payments, and its potential to transform the financial industry. Chapter 8 addresses the criticisms of Ripple and XRP, including centralization, privacy concerns, and environmental impact, and examines Ripple and XRP's response to these criticisms.

Chapter 9 provides an in-depth analysis of the future of Ripple and XRP, including the potential for the ecosystem to disrupt the financial industry, its challenges and opportunities, and its role in shaping the future of money. The conclusion offers a recap of the main points covered in the book, reflects on the significance of Ripple and XRP in the financial industry, and provides final thoughts on the potential of Ripple and XRP to transform the financial landscape.

Overall, this book aims to provide readers with a comprehensive guide to Ripple and XRP, their impact on the financial industry, and their potential for the future. It is suitable for anyone interested in cryptocurrency, blockchain, or the financial industry, including investors, entrepreneurs, academics, and enthusiasts.

Chapter 1: The Birth of Ripple and XRP
Creation of Ripple and XRP

Ripple was founded in 2012 by a group of developers who sought to create a decentralized financial network that could facilitate instant and low-cost cross-border payments. The company's co-founders, Chris Larsen and Jed McCaleb, were both veterans of the tech industry and had previously worked on various projects related to digital currencies.

The idea for Ripple was born out of their frustration with the existing financial system, which they saw as slow, expensive, and prone to errors. They believed that blockchain technology could be used to create a faster and more efficient system for transferring money across borders, and set out to build a platform that could make this vision a reality.

The first iteration of Ripple was actually a digital currency called RipplePay, which was launched in 2005 by Ryan Fugger. RipplePay was designed as a peer-to-peer network for exchanging IOUs, and allowed users to create trust lines with one another to facilitate transactions.

In 2011, Jed McCaleb discovered RipplePay and was inspired by its potential. He reached out to Fugger and proposed the idea of creating a new platform that would use RipplePay as its foundation. Fugger agreed, and together they formed OpenCoin, which would eventually become Ripple.

In 2012, OpenCoin released the first version of the Ripple protocol, which used a consensus algorithm known as

Ripple Protocol Consensus Algorithm (RPCA) to validate transactions. The protocol was designed to allow anyone to issue and exchange any currency, including both traditional fiat currencies and cryptocurrencies, and to facilitate the transfer of value across different networks.

To fund the development of Ripple, the company launched a token sale in 2013, selling XRP tokens to investors in exchange for Bitcoin and other cryptocurrencies. The sale raised over $100 million, making it one of the largest initial coin offerings (ICOs) of its time.

With the funds raised from the token sale, Ripple continued to develop its platform and expand its partnerships with financial institutions around the world. Today, Ripple has become one of the most prominent players in the blockchain and cryptocurrency space, with its XRP token being used by financial institutions to facilitate cross-border payments and other transactions.

The problem Ripple aims to solve

Ripple was founded in 2012 with the aim of solving a significant problem in the traditional financial industry – the inefficiencies and high costs associated with cross-border payments. The traditional system of transferring money across borders is complex, slow, and expensive, with multiple intermediaries involved in the process.

For example, when a person in the US wants to send money to a friend or family member in Europe, the process typically involves multiple banks and financial institutions. The sender's bank may use an intermediary bank, known as a correspondent bank, to facilitate the transfer. The correspondent bank then sends the funds to the recipient's bank, which may use another intermediary bank before finally crediting the funds to the recipient's account. Each intermediary bank may charge a fee for their services, resulting in high costs for the sender and potentially long wait times for the recipient to receive their funds.

Ripple recognized that there was a need for a faster, more efficient, and cost-effective system for cross-border payments. The company's founders believed that blockchain technology could be leveraged to create a new system that would eliminate the need for multiple intermediaries and reduce the time and cost of cross-border transactions.

The traditional system also poses a significant risk to financial institutions due to the time it takes to settle cross-border transactions. During this time, the value of the funds being transferred can fluctuate, leading to potential losses for the financial institutions involved. Ripple's solution aimed to reduce this risk by providing real-time settlement and reducing the time it takes for cross-border transactions to be completed.

Ripple's solution also aimed to address the lack of transparency in the traditional cross-border payment system. Traditional transactions can be opaque, with the sender and recipient having little visibility into the process. Ripple's solution aimed to provide greater transparency by allowing all parties involved in a transaction to view the details of the transaction in real-time.

Overall, Ripple aimed to solve the problems of inefficiency, high cost, risk, and lack of transparency associated with the traditional cross-border payment system. By leveraging blockchain technology, Ripple aimed to create a new system that was faster, more efficient, and cost-effective, while also reducing risk and increasing transparency.

The technology behind Ripple and XRP

Ripple and XRP have gained significant attention in the financial industry due to their innovative technology. To understand the technology behind Ripple and XRP, it is important to first understand the problems they were designed to solve.

As mentioned in the previous section, the traditional cross-border payment system is slow, expensive, and inefficient. It can take days or even weeks to settle a transaction, and the costs associated with sending money across borders can be high due to various fees charged by banks and other financial institutions involved in the process. Additionally, the lack of transparency and security in the current system can create opportunities for fraud and other illegal activities.

To solve these problems, Ripple created a decentralized network that uses blockchain technology to facilitate fast and secure cross-border payments. The technology behind Ripple and XRP is based on a consensus algorithm that ensures transactions are processed quickly and securely.

The Ripple network consists of a series of nodes that work together to validate transactions. When a user initiates a transaction, it is broadcasted to the network, and each node verifies the transaction independently. If the transaction is valid, the nodes reach a consensus and add the transaction to the blockchain.

Unlike traditional blockchain networks, which use Proof of Work (PoW) or Proof of Stake (PoS) algorithms to validate transactions, Ripple uses a unique consensus algorithm known as the Ripple Protocol Consensus Algorithm (RPCA). This algorithm allows the network to process a high volume of transactions quickly and efficiently, without the need for extensive computing power or energy consumption.

The RPCA algorithm uses a process called "voting" to achieve consensus. Each node in the network has a unique list of other nodes it trusts, known as a Unique Node List (UNL). When a transaction is broadcasted, each node checks the transaction against its UNL to determine whether it is valid. If a transaction is deemed valid by a certain percentage of nodes on the UNL, the transaction is added to the blockchain.

In addition to its consensus algorithm, Ripple also uses a unique currency, XRP, to facilitate transactions. XRP is a digital asset that can be used to represent any fiat or cryptocurrency, and it is designed to be a bridge currency that can facilitate transactions between different currencies.

When a user initiates a cross-border payment using Ripple, the sender's currency is converted into XRP, which is then sent across the Ripple network to the receiver's destination currency. The XRP is then converted into the receiver's currency, and the transaction is settled.

Overall, the technology behind Ripple and XRP is designed to solve the problems associated with traditional cross-border payments. By using a decentralized network and a unique consensus algorithm, Ripple can process transactions quickly and efficiently, while also providing increased transparency and security. The use of XRP as a bridge currency also allows for seamless currency conversions, further improving the speed and efficiency of cross-border payments.

Overview of Ripple's founders and team

Ripple was founded in 2012 by Chris Larsen and Jed McCaleb, with the goal of creating a faster, more efficient, and more cost-effective way to transfer money globally. Larsen, a Silicon Valley entrepreneur, had previously co-founded online lending platform E-LOAN and peer-to-peer lending company Prosper Marketplace, while McCaleb was known for creating the file-sharing network eDonkey and the first-ever Bitcoin exchange, Mt. Gox.

After initially working on a Bitcoin-based payment protocol called Ripplepay, Larsen and McCaleb pivoted to develop a new decentralized consensus protocol, which formed the basis of the Ripple network. They were joined by a team of talented engineers, developers, and business professionals, including David Schwartz, Arthur Britto, Stefan Thomas, and Asheesh Birla, among others.

David Schwartz, also known as "JoelKatz," is one of the key figures behind the development of the XRP ledger, Ripple's blockchain technology. Schwartz has been involved in the cryptocurrency space since 2011 and has published several papers on topics ranging from network security to digital currency.

Arthur Britto is another of Ripple's co-founders, who helped develop the Ripple protocol and has contributed to its ongoing development. Britto is also an entrepreneur and software engineer with a background in cryptography and network security.

Stefan Thomas is the former CTO of Ripple and was responsible for the development of the company's technology stack, including the XRP ledger, Interledger protocol, and RippleNet. Thomas has since left Ripple to start his own project called Coil, which aims to revolutionize the way content creators monetize their work.

Asheesh Birla is Ripple's current SVP of Product and Corporate Development and has been with the company since 2013. Birla has played a key role in the development and rollout of RippleNet, which is now used by hundreds of financial institutions around the world.

Together, the founders and team members of Ripple have created a technology platform that has the potential to transform the global financial system. They have brought together their expertise in software development, cryptography, network security, and finance to create a solution that is faster, more efficient, and more cost-effective than traditional payment systems.

Initial reception of Ripple and XRP

Upon its release, Ripple and its digital currency XRP faced a mixed reception from various stakeholders. Some people were skeptical about the new technology, while others saw its potential for revolutionizing the financial industry. This section explores the initial reception of Ripple and XRP and the different reactions that it generated.

One of the key factors that affected the initial reception of Ripple and XRP was the fact that it was launched during a time when cryptocurrencies were still relatively unknown and widely misunderstood. Many people had heard of Bitcoin, but they did not understand the underlying technology that made it possible.

Furthermore, the idea of using digital currencies for cross-border payments was also new, and there was a lack of trust in digital currencies due to concerns about their security and stability.

Despite these challenges, Ripple and XRP were able to generate a significant amount of interest from the financial industry. This was due in part to the fact that the founders of Ripple had a background in finance and were able to speak the language of financial institutions.

As Ripple gained more traction, it became clear that its technology had the potential to solve many of the problems that traditional cross-border payment systems were facing. For example, the traditional system was slow, expensive, and required a complex web of intermediaries to facilitate transactions.

Ripple's technology, on the other hand, was able to facilitate cross-border payments quickly and inexpensively, without the need for intermediaries. This was a game-changer for the financial industry, and it helped to attract many investors and supporters to the Ripple project.

However, not everyone was impressed with Ripple and XRP. Some critics argued that the system was too centralized, as it relied heavily on Ripple Labs to maintain and manage the network. Others raised concerns about the potential for XRP to be used for illegal activities, such as money laundering.

Despite these criticisms, Ripple and XRP continued to gain traction in the financial industry, with many banks and financial institutions expressing interest in the technology. Today, Ripple and XRP are widely recognized as important players in the fintech space, with many experts predicting that they will continue to grow in importance in the years to come.

Chapter 2: The Advantages of XRP
The difference between Ripple and XRP

Ripple is a financial technology company that provides solutions for global payments. Its products include RippleNet, a global network of banks and financial institutions, and On-Demand Liquidity (ODL), a service that enables instant cross-border payments using digital assets. XRP is the digital asset used in the ODL service and is often associated with Ripple. However, there are some significant differences between Ripple and XRP.

Firstly, Ripple is a company that develops technology solutions for cross-border payments, whereas XRP is a digital asset that facilitates the movement of value across the RippleNet network. Ripple provides the infrastructure, and XRP provides the liquidity. The RippleNet network is a decentralized network of financial institutions that use Ripple's technology to facilitate instant cross-border payments. XRP is the digital asset that is used as a bridge currency in these transactions.

Secondly, Ripple is not the only company that uses XRP. Other companies can also use XRP to facilitate cross-border payments. This means that XRP is not exclusive to Ripple, and anyone can use it. XRP can be purchased on various cryptocurrency exchanges and can be used to facilitate cross-border payments.

Thirdly, the value of XRP is not directly linked to the success of Ripple as a company. The value of XRP is determined by market forces, and its price can fluctuate based on supply and demand. The success of Ripple as a company does not necessarily translate to the success of XRP as a digital asset.

Lastly, Ripple and XRP are not the same thing. Ripple is a company that develops technology solutions for cross-border payments, and XRP is a digital asset that facilitates the movement of value across the RippleNet network. While Ripple and XRP are often associated with each other, they are two separate entities with different functions.

In summary, Ripple and XRP are not the same thing. Ripple is a company that develops technology solutions for cross-border payments, and XRP is a digital asset that facilitates the movement of value across the RippleNet network. While Ripple and XRP are often associated with each other, they are two separate entities with different functions.

The benefits of using XRP in cross-border payments

Cross-border payments have been a challenge for traditional financial institutions due to several factors such as high transaction costs, slow processing times, and lack of interoperability between different payment systems. The emergence of blockchain technology, and specifically XRP, has provided solutions to these challenges, making cross-border payments faster, cheaper, and more efficient.

One of the main advantages of using XRP in cross-border payments is its speed. XRP transactions are processed within seconds, unlike traditional payment methods that may take several days to complete. This is because XRP transactions do not require the same level of intermediaries and verification as traditional payment systems. Transactions are validated by a network of trusted nodes, which reduces the time and cost associated with traditional payment processing.

Another advantage of XRP is its low transaction fees. Traditional payment methods involve several intermediaries, each charging a fee for their services. These fees add up, resulting in high transaction costs, especially for cross-border payments. With XRP, transaction fees are significantly lower due to the absence of intermediaries, making it a more cost-effective option for cross-border payments.

XRP also offers greater efficiency in cross-border payments. This is due to the fact that XRP is a decentralized digital asset that can be used on any platform. It is not restricted by the limitations of traditional payment systems that are often incompatible with each other. Therefore, XRP can be used to facilitate cross-border payments across different payment systems, which increases efficiency and reduces costs.

In addition, XRP provides greater transparency and security in cross-border payments. Blockchain technology ensures that transactions are immutable and transparent, making it easier to trace and verify transactions. This reduces the risk of fraud and ensures that funds are transferred securely and without the risk of tampering.

Overall, the benefits of using XRP in cross-border payments are significant. Its speed, low transaction fees, interoperability, and transparency make it an ideal option for financial institutions looking to improve their cross-border payment processes. As more institutions adopt XRP, it is likely that cross-border payments will become faster, cheaper, and more efficient.

The speed and cost-effectiveness of XRP transactions

One of the key advantages of XRP is its speed and cost-effectiveness in processing cross-border transactions. Traditional methods of international payments often require multiple intermediaries, resulting in longer processing times and higher fees. In contrast, XRP transactions are designed to be almost instantaneous and significantly less expensive.

Speed of XRP transactions

One of the reasons for the speed of XRP transactions is its consensus algorithm. Unlike other cryptocurrencies that use a proof-of-work system, XRP uses a unique consensus algorithm known as the XRP Ledger Consensus Protocol. This protocol allows for faster transaction processing times, with transactions taking only a few seconds to complete.

In addition, the XRP Ledger is capable of handling a high volume of transactions per second. It is estimated that the ledger can process up to 1,500 transactions per second, which is significantly higher than other cryptocurrencies, such as Bitcoin, which can process around 7 transactions per second.

Cost-effectiveness of XRP transactions

Another significant advantage of XRP transactions is its cost-effectiveness. Traditional international payments often involve several intermediaries, each charging a fee for their services. These fees can add up quickly, resulting in high transaction costs for the sender and recipient.

In contrast, XRP transactions have a significantly lower transaction cost. The cost of an XRP transaction is measured in "drops," with one drop being a millionth of a single XRP. The current cost of an XRP transaction is 0.00001 XRP per transaction, which is a fraction of a penny.

Furthermore, because XRP transactions do not require intermediaries, the cost of transactions can be significantly lower than traditional methods. This can lead to lower transaction costs for both the sender and recipient, making XRP an attractive option for cross-border payments.

In conclusion, the speed and cost-effectiveness of XRP transactions make it an appealing alternative to traditional international payment methods. The XRP Ledger Consensus Protocol allows for almost instantaneous transaction processing times, while the low transaction cost can lead to significant savings for both the sender and recipient. These benefits are why many businesses and financial institutions are considering the adoption of XRP for their cross-border payment needs.

The role of XRP as a bridge currency

In traditional cross-border payments, two banks in different countries need to have a pre-existing relationship or rely on a correspondent bank to facilitate the transfer of funds between them. This process can be time-consuming and costly, often involving multiple intermediaries and fees. However, with the use of XRP as a bridge currency, cross-border payments can be made faster, cheaper, and more efficiently.

What is a Bridge Currency?

A bridge currency is a digital asset that facilitates the exchange between two different currencies, allowing transactions to occur without the need for a direct exchange between the two. XRP serves as a bridge currency for cross-border payments on the Ripple network, enabling the movement of funds between different fiat currencies.

How XRP Works as a Bridge Currency:

When two banks want to exchange currencies using the Ripple network, XRP is used as a bridge currency between them. For example, if a bank in the United States wants to send money to a bank in Japan, the U.S. dollars are converted into XRP, and the XRP is then transferred to the Japanese bank. The Japanese bank then converts the XRP into Japanese yen.

Benefits of XRP as a Bridge Currency:

Speed:

The use of XRP as a bridge currency enables cross-border payments to be settled in a matter of seconds, compared to the days or even weeks it can take with traditional methods. This is because XRP transactions are processed almost instantly on the Ripple network, making it an ideal solution for time-sensitive transactions.

Cost-Effective:

Using XRP as a bridge currency eliminates the need for multiple intermediaries, reducing the fees associated with cross-border payments. This can result in significant cost savings for both banks and their customers.

Liquidity:

XRP's use as a bridge currency creates a liquid market for the digital asset, increasing its value and improving its utility. As more financial institutions adopt the Ripple network and use XRP for cross-border payments, the demand for the digital asset increases, leading to increased liquidity and potentially driving up its value.

Accessibility:

The use of XRP as a bridge currency allows banks and financial institutions to make cross-border payments to countries that may not have a direct banking relationship. This increases the accessibility of cross-border payments and opens up new markets for businesses and individuals.

Conclusion:

XRP's use as a bridge currency on the Ripple network has the potential to revolutionize the cross-border payment industry. Its speed, cost-effectiveness, liquidity, and accessibility make it an attractive solution for banks and financial institutions looking to streamline their cross-border payment processes. As more institutions adopt the Ripple network and use XRP as a bridge currency, it is likely to become an even more integral part of the global financial system.

The scalability of XRP compared to other cryptocurrencies

The scalability of a cryptocurrency is an important factor to consider when evaluating its potential for widespread adoption and use. Scalability refers to the ability of a cryptocurrency to handle a large volume of transactions quickly and efficiently without compromising its security and decentralization. In this section, we will examine the scalability of XRP compared to other cryptocurrencies.

Bitcoin, the first cryptocurrency, was designed to have a maximum block size of 1 MB, which limits its transaction processing capacity to a few transactions per second. Ethereum, another popular cryptocurrency, can handle around 15 transactions per second. In comparison, XRP has a much higher transaction processing capacity, with the ability to handle up to 1,500 transactions per second.

One of the reasons for XRP's superior scalability is its use of a consensus algorithm called the Ripple Protocol Consensus Algorithm (RPCA). Unlike the proof-of-work algorithm used by Bitcoin and other cryptocurrencies, the RPCA algorithm does not require miners to solve complex mathematical equations to validate transactions. Instead, it uses a network of trusted nodes to reach consensus on the state of the network.

Another factor that contributes to XRP's scalability is its use of a distributed ledger technology called the XRP Ledger.

The XRP Ledger is a decentralized ledger that maintains a record of all XRP transactions. It is designed to be highly efficient and scalable, with the ability to handle thousands of transactions per second.

XRP's scalability is also enhanced by its ability to settle transactions quickly. Unlike traditional cross-border payments, which can take several days to complete, XRP transactions settle in a matter of seconds. This is because XRP transactions do not need to be processed through multiple intermediaries, which can introduce delays and increase transaction costs.

In addition, XRP's scalability is further improved by its low transaction fees. The cost of sending XRP is significantly lower than the fees charged by traditional financial institutions for cross-border payments. This makes XRP an attractive option for businesses and individuals looking to save money on transaction fees.

Overall, XRP's superior scalability makes it an attractive option for businesses and individuals looking to conduct fast, cost-effective, and scalable cross-border payments. As more businesses and financial institutions adopt XRP, its scalability is likely to become even more important, making it a key factor in its continued success and adoption.

Chapter 3: The Adoption of Ripple and XRP
The early adopters of Ripple and XRP

In the early days of Ripple and XRP, the technology and digital asset were met with skepticism and faced significant challenges in gaining traction in the financial industry. However, as the benefits and potential of the technology became more widely recognized, more companies began to adopt Ripple and XRP as a solution to their cross-border payment needs.

This section will explore some of the early adopters of Ripple and XRP and how they integrated the technology into their business models.

Santander

In 2015, Santander became one of the first major banks to adopt Ripple and XRP for cross-border payments. The Spanish bank launched a mobile app called OnePay FX that uses Ripple's technology to enable near-instant international payments in multiple currencies. The app was initially available to Santander's customers in Spain, the UK, Brazil, and Poland, and has since expanded to other countries.

Santander's adoption of Ripple and XRP was significant because it demonstrated the potential of the technology to revolutionize the traditional banking industry. The bank was able to reduce the time and cost of cross-border payments while improving transparency and security.

American Express

American Express (Amex) is another early adopter of Ripple and XRP. In 2017, the company announced a partnership with Ripple to explore how blockchain technology could be used to improve the speed and efficiency of its cross-border payments. The partnership allowed Amex to process non-card payments to the UK from the US in a matter of seconds, compared to the several days it would typically take.

Amex's adoption of Ripple and XRP highlights the benefits of the technology for businesses that require fast and secure cross-border payments. The partnership with Ripple also helped to increase the credibility of the technology and its potential for wider adoption.

MoneyGram

MoneyGram is a global money transfer company that has been in operation for over 80 years. In 2018, the company announced a partnership with Ripple that would allow it to use XRP for cross-border payments. The partnership was significant because it demonstrated the potential for digital assets like XRP to improve the speed and cost-effectiveness of cross-border payments for businesses and consumers.

MoneyGram's adoption of XRP allowed the company to settle transactions in a matter of seconds, compared to the several minutes it would typically take. The use of XRP also helped to reduce the cost of cross-border payments for MoneyGram and its customers.

Conclusion:

The early adopters of Ripple and XRP played a significant role in demonstrating the potential of the technology for the financial industry. Their adoption of the technology helped to increase awareness and credibility and paved the way for wider adoption by other companies. As more businesses begin to recognize the benefits of Ripple and XRP, we can expect to see further growth in the adoption of the technology in the coming years.

The current state of Ripple's adoption in the financial industry

The adoption of Ripple and XRP in the financial industry has been steadily increasing since their inception in 2012. While the early days were marked by skepticism and uncertainty, many financial institutions and companies have recognized the potential benefits of using Ripple's technology and XRP as a bridge currency.

As of 2023, Ripple has partnered with over 300 financial institutions and payment providers worldwide, including some of the largest banks and payment processors in the world. These partnerships allow these institutions to utilize Ripple's payment protocol and take advantage of the benefits that come with it, such as faster and more cost-effective cross-border payments.

One of the key factors driving Ripple's adoption is the need for faster and more efficient cross-border payments. With traditional payment methods, international payments can take days to settle and involve multiple intermediaries, leading to higher costs and increased risk of fraud or errors. Ripple's technology, on the other hand, allows for near-instant settlement times and eliminates the need for intermediaries, making payments faster and cheaper.

Another factor contributing to Ripple's adoption is its focus on compliance and regulatory transparency. Ripple has worked closely with regulators around the world to ensure that its technology and payment protocol adhere to legal and regulatory standards. This has helped to build trust with financial institutions and payment providers, who are often subject to strict regulations and compliance requirements.

In addition to partnerships with financial institutions, Ripple has also gained adoption in other industries, such as remittance and e-commerce. Many remittance companies have turned to Ripple's technology as a way to offer faster and cheaper international payments to their customers, while e-commerce platforms have integrated XRP as a payment option, allowing customers to make purchases using the digital currency.

Despite its growing adoption, Ripple still faces challenges in achieving widespread acceptance in the financial industry. Some institutions remain hesitant to adopt new technology and digital currencies, while others may be reluctant to work with Ripple due to its association with XRP, which has faced regulatory scrutiny in the past. However, with the continued growth and success of Ripple's partnerships and technology, it is likely that adoption will continue to increase in the years to come.

The benefits of adopting Ripple and XRP for financial institutions

Financial institutions that adopt Ripple and XRP stand to benefit in several ways. Here are some of the key advantages of adopting Ripple and XRP for financial institutions:

Faster and Cheaper Cross-border Payments: One of the most significant benefits of adopting Ripple and XRP is that financial institutions can offer faster and cheaper cross-border payments to their customers. With traditional cross-border payment methods, such as SWIFT, it can take several days for a transaction to clear, and the fees can be high. However, with Ripple and XRP, transactions can be settled in a matter of seconds, and the fees are a fraction of what traditional methods charge.

Enhanced Security: Another benefit of adopting Ripple and XRP is enhanced security. Ripple uses a decentralized ledger technology to secure transactions, making it much more secure than traditional payment methods. Furthermore, Ripple and XRP use advanced cryptography to protect against fraud and other malicious activities.

Increased Efficiency: Ripple and XRP can help financial institutions increase efficiency in their operations. By using a decentralized ledger technology, Ripple eliminates the need for intermediaries, which can help streamline the payment process and reduce costs. Additionally, Ripple's software can integrate with existing payment systems, making it easier for financial institutions to adopt the technology.

Access to New Markets: By adopting Ripple and XRP, financial institutions can gain access to new markets that were previously inaccessible due to regulatory or infrastructure barriers. Ripple has partnerships with several banks and financial institutions around the world, which can help expand a financial institution's reach.

Competitive Advantage: Finally, adopting Ripple and XRP can give financial institutions a competitive advantage in the marketplace. By offering faster, cheaper, and more secure cross-border payments, financial institutions can differentiate themselves from their competitors and attract more customers.

In conclusion, adopting Ripple and XRP can offer numerous benefits to financial institutions, including faster and cheaper cross-border payments, enhanced security, increased efficiency, access to new markets, and a competitive advantage in the marketplace.

Challenges in the adoption of Ripple and XRP

As with any new technology, Ripple and XRP have faced several challenges in their adoption by financial institutions. These challenges include regulatory hurdles, lack of understanding of the technology, and resistance to change.

One of the primary challenges in the adoption of Ripple and XRP is the regulatory environment. Ripple's decentralized structure and the use of XRP as a bridge currency between fiat currencies can create confusion and raise concerns for regulators. The lack of clarity around the regulatory status of Ripple and XRP has made some financial institutions hesitant to adopt the technology.

Another challenge is the lack of understanding of the technology. Ripple and XRP use a unique consensus mechanism called the Ripple Protocol Consensus Algorithm (RPCA), which is different from the Proof of Work (PoW) and Proof of Stake (PoS) mechanisms used by other cryptocurrencies. The unfamiliarity with RPCA and its advantages can make it difficult for financial institutions to fully understand the benefits of Ripple and XRP.

Additionally, financial institutions are often resistant to change, particularly when it comes to their core systems and processes. The integration of Ripple and XRP can require significant changes to existing systems and processes, which can be a daunting task for many institutions.

Another challenge is the lack of liquidity in certain markets. While Ripple and XRP have made significant strides in gaining adoption in major markets, there are still areas where liquidity is limited. This can make it difficult for financial institutions to use Ripple and XRP for cross-border transactions in these markets.

Despite these challenges, Ripple and XRP have continued to make progress in their adoption by financial institutions. The company has established partnerships with several major financial institutions, including Santander, Standard Chartered, and American Express. These partnerships have helped to increase the visibility of Ripple and XRP and demonstrate their potential to transform cross-border payments.

Furthermore, Ripple has been working with regulators to address concerns around the regulatory status of Ripple and XRP. The company has established a regulatory affairs team to engage with policymakers and ensure that the technology is compliant with applicable laws and regulations.

In conclusion, the adoption of Ripple and XRP by financial institutions is not without its challenges. However, the technology has demonstrated significant potential to transform cross-border payments and increase efficiency in the financial industry. As the regulatory environment becomes clearer and financial institutions become more familiar with the technology, it is likely that we will see increased adoption of Ripple and XRP in the coming years.

Future prospects for the adoption of Ripple and XRP

Despite the challenges, the future of Ripple and XRP looks promising. Ripple's unique position in the cross-border payments space, its partnerships with financial institutions and payment providers, and its growing ecosystem all point to a bright future for the company and its digital asset XRP.

One of the key factors that will drive the adoption of Ripple and XRP in the future is the increasing demand for cross-border payments. As the global economy becomes more interconnected, the need for fast, reliable, and cost-effective cross-border payments will only continue to grow. Ripple's technology and XRP provide a solution to this problem, offering near-instant settlement times and significantly lower costs compared to traditional payment methods.

Another factor that will drive the adoption of Ripple and XRP is the increasing interest from financial institutions and payment providers. Ripple's partnerships with major banks and payment providers such as Santander, Standard Chartered, and MoneyGram have helped to legitimize the company and its technology in the eyes of the financial industry. As more institutions and providers recognize the benefits of Ripple's technology and XRP, we can expect to see increased adoption of these solutions.

In addition, Ripple's growing ecosystem of developers and entrepreneurs is also contributing to the future prospects for the adoption of Ripple and XRP. Ripple's open-source technology and APIs allow developers to build innovative new applications and services that leverage Ripple's network and XRP. This growing ecosystem is helping to drive innovation in the cross-border payments space and could lead to new use cases and applications for Ripple and XRP.

Despite these positive signs, there are still challenges to be overcome in the adoption of Ripple and XRP. One major challenge is regulatory uncertainty, particularly in the United States. The SEC's ongoing lawsuit against Ripple has created uncertainty for investors and may make some financial institutions hesitant to adopt Ripple's technology or XRP. However, there are signs that this regulatory uncertainty may be easing, with the recent settlement of a similar lawsuit against Ripple by the U.S. Department of Justice.

Another challenge is competition from other cross-border payment solutions and digital assets. While Ripple and XRP offer significant advantages over traditional payment methods, there are other solutions and digital assets that are also vying for a share of the cross-border payments market. As the market becomes more crowded, Ripple will need to continue to innovate and differentiate itself in order to stay ahead.

In conclusion, the adoption of Ripple and XRP is still in its early stages, but the future looks promising. As the global economy becomes more interconnected and the demand for cross-border payments grows, Ripple's unique position in the market and its growing ecosystem of developers and entrepreneurs will help to drive adoption of its technology and XRP. However, there are still challenges to be overcome, particularly in the regulatory environment and competition from other solutions and digital assets.

Chapter 4: Ripple and XRP in the Cryptocurrency Market

Ripple's role in the cryptocurrency market

Ripple and its native cryptocurrency XRP have a unique position in the cryptocurrency market. Unlike most other cryptocurrencies, which were created with the intention of serving as a decentralized alternative to traditional currencies, Ripple was designed to improve the speed and efficiency of cross-border payments for financial institutions.

As a result, Ripple and XRP have often been viewed as a "hybrid" between traditional finance and cryptocurrency. This has led to some controversy and criticism within the cryptocurrency community, with some arguing that Ripple is not a "real" cryptocurrency because it is not fully decentralized.

Despite this criticism, Ripple has managed to establish itself as one of the most valuable cryptocurrencies in the market, with a current market cap of over $30 billion. Its value has been buoyed by a number of factors, including its partnerships with major financial institutions, its growing adoption in the cross-border payments space, and its unique features compared to other cryptocurrencies.

One of the key advantages of Ripple is its ability to settle transactions in real-time. This is made possible through its use of the XRP Ledger, which is capable of processing up to 1,500 transactions per second. This is significantly faster than other cryptocurrencies like Bitcoin and Ethereum, which can take several minutes or even hours to settle transactions.

Another advantage of Ripple is its ability to facilitate cross-border payments without the need for intermediaries like banks. This is accomplished through its use of RippleNet, a global network of financial institutions that use Ripple's technology to facilitate cross-border payments. By eliminating the need for intermediaries, Ripple is able to reduce transaction costs and increase the speed and efficiency of cross-border payments.

Ripple has also been successful in attracting partnerships with major financial institutions, including American Express, Santander, and Standard Chartered. These partnerships have helped to increase the visibility and legitimacy of Ripple in the financial industry, as well as provide a platform for Ripple to showcase the benefits of its technology.

Despite its success, Ripple has faced some challenges in the cryptocurrency market. One of the main criticisms of Ripple is its centralized nature, with some arguing that its control over the supply of XRP makes it more akin to a traditional company than a decentralized cryptocurrency. This has led to some concerns over its long-term viability and potential for regulatory scrutiny.

Overall, Ripple's unique position in the cryptocurrency market as a hybrid between traditional finance and cryptocurrency has allowed it to carve out a significant market share. While it may face challenges from critics who question its decentralized nature, its partnerships with major financial institutions and growing adoption in the cross-border payments space suggest that Ripple and XRP have a promising future in the financial industry.

Comparison of XRP with other cryptocurrencies

As one of the top cryptocurrencies in the market, XRP is often compared to other digital assets such as Bitcoin and Ethereum. In this section, we will explore the similarities and differences between XRP and other popular cryptocurrencies.

Bitcoin vs. XRP:

Bitcoin, the first and most well-known cryptocurrency, was created in 2009 as a decentralized digital currency with the aim of providing an alternative to traditional banking systems. It uses a proof-of-work consensus algorithm to validate transactions on its blockchain network. One of the key differences between Bitcoin and XRP is their purpose. While Bitcoin is primarily used as a medium of exchange and a store of value, XRP was designed specifically for use in cross-border payments.

In terms of transaction speed and cost, XRP has a clear advantage over Bitcoin. Bitcoin's block time is around 10 minutes, meaning transactions can take up to an hour to be confirmed. In contrast, XRP transactions are processed almost instantly, with settlement times of just a few seconds. Additionally, Bitcoin transaction fees can be high during times of high network congestion, whereas XRP transaction fees are significantly lower.

Ethereum vs. XRP:

Ethereum, launched in 2015, is a decentralized platform that enables developers to build and deploy decentralized applications (dapps) on its blockchain network. Ethereum uses a proof-of-work consensus algorithm similar to Bitcoin, but is in the process of transitioning to a proof-of-stake algorithm. While Ethereum and XRP are both cryptocurrencies, their use cases are quite different.

Like Bitcoin, Ethereum transactions can be slow and expensive, with confirmation times ranging from a few minutes to several hours depending on network congestion. XRP, on the other hand, offers nearly instant settlement times and low transaction fees. Additionally, while Ethereum has a wide range of use cases beyond just payments, XRP's focus is primarily on facilitating cross-border payments.

Stellar vs. XRP:

Stellar is another cryptocurrency that was designed specifically for cross-border payments. Launched in 2014, Stellar's network operates similarly to Ripple's, using a consensus algorithm called Stellar Consensus Protocol (SCP) to validate transactions. Like XRP, Stellar transactions settle quickly and are relatively inexpensive.

One key difference between the two is their distribution model. Ripple Labs holds the majority of XRP tokens in circulation, while Stellar's tokens are distributed through a non-profit organization called the Stellar Development Foundation. Additionally, while Ripple primarily targets financial institutions, Stellar aims to provide financial services to individuals in developing countries who lack access to traditional banking systems.

Overall, XRP's speed and low transaction costs make it an attractive option for cross-border payments, particularly for financial institutions. While it may not have the same broad range of use cases as Ethereum or the same distribution model as Stellar, its targeted focus and efficiency make it a valuable player in the cryptocurrency market.

The impact of Ripple and XRP on the cryptocurrency industry

Ripple and XRP have had a significant impact on the cryptocurrency industry since their inception in 2012. Here, we will explore the impact of Ripple and XRP on the cryptocurrency industry and how they have influenced the development of the industry.

Increasing Institutional Interest

Ripple's focus on developing a blockchain-based payment solution for financial institutions has attracted the attention of many large financial players. This has led to an increase in institutional interest in cryptocurrencies, which has traditionally been dominated by retail investors. The adoption of Ripple and XRP by financial institutions has demonstrated the potential for cryptocurrencies to be used as a legitimate payment solution.

Improved Scalability

One of the primary issues facing cryptocurrencies is scalability. As more users enter the network, the time and cost required for transactions to be processed increases. Ripple's use of the XRP Ledger, which can handle up to 1,500 transactions per second, has demonstrated the potential for cryptocurrencies to handle large-scale transactions.

Increased Liquidity

The adoption of XRP by financial institutions has led to an increase in liquidity for the cryptocurrency. This has helped to stabilize the value of XRP and has made it a more attractive investment for traders and investors.

Greater Adoption of Interoperability

Ripple's focus on interoperability has influenced the cryptocurrency industry to adopt more open standards. This has led to greater collaboration between different cryptocurrency projects and has helped to create a more unified and cohesive industry.

Ripple as a Challenger to Traditional Payment Systems

Ripple's focus on providing a faster, cheaper, and more efficient payment system has positioned it as a potential challenger to traditional payment systems such as SWIFT. This has led to increased competition in the payment industry and has forced traditional players to improve their services.

Regulation

Ripple's adoption by financial institutions has led to greater scrutiny from regulators. This has forced Ripple to become more compliant with existing regulations and has helped to create a more regulated cryptocurrency industry.

Criticisms and Controversies

Despite its many benefits, Ripple and XRP have faced criticisms and controversies. One of the primary criticisms is the centralization of the XRP Ledger, which is controlled by Ripple. Additionally, Ripple has faced several lawsuits related to the sale of XRP as an unregistered security.

In conclusion, Ripple and XRP have had a significant impact on the cryptocurrency industry. Their focus on providing a faster, cheaper, and more efficient payment system has attracted the attention of financial institutions and has demonstrated the potential for cryptocurrencies to be used as a legitimate payment solution. Additionally, their use of the XRP Ledger has demonstrated the potential for cryptocurrencies to handle large-scale transactions. However, Ripple and XRP have also faced criticisms and controversies, highlighting the challenges that exist in the cryptocurrency industry.

The controversy surrounding Ripple and XRP

Ripple and its native cryptocurrency, XRP, have been at the center of controversy in the cryptocurrency industry since their inception. The controversies surrounding Ripple and XRP have been due to their perceived lack of decentralization, regulatory issues, and lawsuits. This section will discuss the controversies surrounding Ripple and XRP.

The Decentralization Controversy

One of the main controversies surrounding Ripple and XRP is their perceived lack of decentralization. Unlike Bitcoin and other cryptocurrencies, which are designed to be decentralized, Ripple and XRP are more centralized. Ripple Labs, the company behind Ripple, holds a significant amount of XRP and has control over its distribution. Moreover, the Ripple network requires a set of trusted validators to confirm transactions, which some argue is a centralization point.

Critics argue that Ripple and XRP's centralization undermines the principles of decentralization, which is one of the core tenets of the cryptocurrency industry. They claim that Ripple's centralized nature gives it the power to manipulate the XRP price and influence the network's operation.

On the other hand, Ripple and XRP proponents argue that the centralization is necessary to ensure scalability and security in the network. They claim that Ripple's centralized structure allows for faster transaction speeds and lower transaction fees, making it more suitable for use in the financial industry.

Regulatory Issues

Another source of controversy surrounding Ripple and XRP is their regulatory issues. Ripple has faced regulatory challenges from various jurisdictions around the world, primarily due to the company's alleged violations of securities laws.

The controversy began in 2018 when the U.S. Securities and Exchange Commission (SEC) filed a lawsuit against Ripple, alleging that the company had conducted an unregistered securities offering by selling XRP tokens to investors. The lawsuit claims that Ripple's sales of XRP were a part of an ongoing offering of securities that began in 2013 and has raised over $1.3 billion in total.

The lawsuit has put Ripple and XRP's legal status in limbo, as the SEC's lawsuit argues that XRP is a security, while Ripple maintains that it is a digital asset. If the court rules that XRP is a security, Ripple may face penalties, and XRP may become subject to more stringent regulatory requirements.

Lawsuits

Apart from the SEC lawsuit, Ripple and XRP have been involved in other legal battles. In 2019, a group of XRP investors filed a class-action lawsuit against Ripple, claiming that the company had sold XRP as an unregistered security. The lawsuit argues that Ripple's sale of XRP was a violation of securities laws, and the investors seek compensation for their losses.

In 2020, the U.S. District Court dismissed the lawsuit, stating that the plaintiffs had failed to provide evidence that their losses were directly caused by Ripple's actions. However, the plaintiffs filed an amended complaint, and the lawsuit is ongoing.

Apart from the class-action lawsuit, Ripple is also facing a lawsuit filed by the U.S. SEC alleging that the company and its executives sold unregistered securities. The lawsuit is ongoing, and its outcome could have significant implications for the regulatory status of XRP and Ripple's future.

Conclusion

The controversies surrounding Ripple and XRP have been ongoing since their inception. The centralization controversy, regulatory issues, and lawsuits have put Ripple and XRP's legal and regulatory status in limbo. While some argue that Ripple and XRP's centralization is necessary for scalability and security, critics argue that it undermines the principles of decentralization. Moreover, Ripple's regulatory issues and lawsuits have added to the uncertainty surrounding the future of Ripple and XRP.

The future of Ripple and XRP in the cryptocurrency market

Ripple and its digital asset, XRP, have been at the center of numerous controversies and debates in the cryptocurrency market. While the company has been successful in establishing partnerships with financial institutions for cross-border payments, XRP's position as the third-largest cryptocurrency by market capitalization has not been without its challenges. In this section, we will explore the future of Ripple and XRP in the cryptocurrency market and the various factors that will shape their trajectory.

The Evolution of Ripple and XRP

Ripple has come a long way since its inception in 2012. From the early days of developing a payment protocol to its current status as a blockchain-based payment system used by banks and payment providers worldwide, Ripple has had a significant impact on the financial industry. Similarly, XRP has seen significant growth since its launch in 2013, with its market capitalization reaching an all-time high of over $140 billion in 2018.

One of the most notable developments in the evolution of Ripple and XRP has been the company's pivot towards providing software solutions to financial institutions. This approach has allowed Ripple to establish partnerships with banks and payment providers worldwide, including American Express, Santander, and Standard Chartered. These partnerships have enabled the use of XRP as a bridge currency in cross-border payments, reducing transaction times and costs significantly.

Another significant development has been Ripple's focus on regulatory compliance. In recent years, the company has taken steps to ensure that its operations comply with regulatory requirements, which has helped to build trust among financial institutions and investors. The company's efforts have paid off, with regulators in countries such as Japan and the United Arab Emirates granting Ripple licenses to operate in their jurisdictions.

The Future of Ripple and XRP

The future of Ripple and XRP in the cryptocurrency market will be shaped by several factors. These include:

Regulation: As with any cryptocurrency, the regulatory environment will play a crucial role in the future of Ripple and XRP. While Ripple has made significant progress in regulatory compliance, ongoing legal disputes with the US Securities and Exchange Commission (SEC) regarding XRP's classification as a security have cast a shadow over the company's future.

Competition: Ripple's success in the cross-border payments space has attracted competition from established players such as SWIFT, as well as other blockchain-based payment systems such as Stellar. To maintain its position as a market leader, Ripple will need to continue to innovate and provide value to its customers.

Adoption: While Ripple has established partnerships with several financial institutions, adoption of its payment system and XRP as a bridge currency has been slow. As more institutions and individuals adopt cryptocurrencies, Ripple and XRP will need to position themselves to take advantage of the growing market.

Technology: Ripple's payment protocol and XRP's consensus algorithm have been the subject of much debate and criticism within the cryptocurrency community. As the technology continues to evolve, Ripple and XRP will need to keep pace with developments and ensure that their systems remain secure and efficient.

Conclusion

Ripple and XRP have come a long way since their inception, with the former developing a blockchain-based payment system used by financial institutions worldwide, and the latter becoming the third-largest cryptocurrency by market capitalization. Despite its success, Ripple and XRP face challenges such as regulatory uncertainty and competition from established players and other blockchain-based payment systems.

However, if Ripple can navigate these challenges and continue to provide value to its customers, the future of Ripple and XRP in the cryptocurrency market looks promising. As more financial institutions and individuals adopt cryptocurrencies, the demand for efficient cross-border payment systems such as Ripple will only increase, providing ample opportunities for growth and development.

Chapter 5: The Ripple Community
Overview of the Ripple community

The Ripple community is a diverse group of individuals, organizations, and businesses that are united by a common interest in the Ripple network and its associated products, including the XRP digital currency. This community has grown rapidly since the launch of the Ripple network in 2012, and today it includes a wide range of participants from around the world.

At its core, the Ripple community is made up of individuals who are interested in the potential of blockchain technology to revolutionize the financial industry. Many members of the community are early adopters of cryptocurrencies and blockchain technology, and they see Ripple as a powerful tool for facilitating faster, cheaper, and more secure cross-border payments.

In addition to individuals, the Ripple community also includes a growing number of businesses and organizations that are working to integrate Ripple's technology into their operations. These range from small startups to major financial institutions, and they are all united by a shared commitment to leveraging Ripple's technology to create more efficient and effective financial systems.

One of the key features of the Ripple community is its open and collaborative nature. Members of the community are encouraged to share ideas, provide feedback, and work together to improve the Ripple network and its associated products. This has led to the development of a wide range of tools and resources that are designed to help users get the most out of the Ripple network, including online forums, social media groups, and developer communities.

Another important aspect of the Ripple community is its commitment to education and outreach. Many members of the community are actively involved in spreading the word about Ripple and its potential to transform the financial industry. This includes speaking at conferences, hosting meetups and workshops, and engaging with media outlets to raise awareness about Ripple and its products.

Overall, the Ripple community is a vibrant and dynamic group of individuals, businesses, and organizations that are united by a shared vision of using blockchain technology to create a more efficient and effective financial system. As Ripple continues to grow and evolve, this community will undoubtedly play an important role in shaping its future direction and helping to ensure that it remains at the forefront of innovation in the blockchain industry.

The role of the community in Ripple's success

The Ripple community has played a significant role in the success of the company and its products, including XRP. The community has been instrumental in promoting Ripple's vision of creating a more efficient and cost-effective global payment system.

One of the key ways that the community has contributed to Ripple's success is through their support of the company's products and services. The community has been active in promoting Ripple and XRP on social media, forums, and other online platforms. This has helped to increase awareness of Ripple and its products, which has in turn led to greater adoption and usage of XRP.

In addition to promoting Ripple and XRP, the community has also been active in developing tools and applications that leverage the Ripple network. This includes the development of wallets, exchanges, and other financial applications that support XRP and other cryptocurrencies. These tools and applications have made it easier for people to use XRP and other cryptocurrencies, which has helped to increase adoption and usage.

The community has also been active in supporting Ripple's mission of creating a more inclusive financial system. This includes efforts to promote financial inclusion and support for marginalized communities around the world. For example, Ripple has partnered with organizations such as the Bill and

Melinda Gates Foundation and Mercy Corps to support financial inclusion initiatives in developing countries.

The Ripple community has also been instrumental in advocating for regulatory clarity around cryptocurrencies and blockchain technology. This includes efforts to engage with regulators and policymakers to promote greater understanding of the potential benefits of cryptocurrencies and blockchain technology. The community has also worked to develop industry standards and best practices to promote greater transparency and accountability in the cryptocurrency industry.

Overall, the Ripple community has played a vital role in promoting Ripple's vision of creating a more efficient and inclusive global payment system. Through their support of Ripple and XRP, as well as their development of tools and applications that leverage the Ripple network, the community has helped to drive adoption and usage of XRP, while also promoting greater financial inclusion and regulatory clarity around cryptocurrencies and blockchain technology. As Ripple continues to grow and expand its reach, the community will no doubt play an even greater role in shaping the future of the global payment system.

The development of the Ripple ecosystem

The development of the Ripple ecosystem has been a key factor in the success of Ripple and XRP. The Ripple ecosystem consists of various components, including the RippleNet, the XRP Ledger, and the Interledger Protocol. Each of these components plays a vital role in facilitating cross-border payments and enabling the adoption of Ripple and XRP.

RippleNet is a network of financial institutions and payment providers that use Ripple's software solutions to facilitate cross-border payments. The network currently includes over 300 customers, including banks, payment providers, and remittance companies. RippleNet enables these institutions to make faster and cheaper cross-border payments, improving the overall efficiency of the global payments system.

The XRP Ledger is a decentralized digital asset exchange and settlement platform. It is designed to provide fast, secure, and low-cost transactions, making it ideal for cross-border payments. The ledger uses a consensus algorithm called the XRP Ledger Consensus Protocol to validate transactions and prevent double-spending. It also has a built-in decentralized exchange that allows users to trade XRP and other digital assets.

The Interledger Protocol (ILP) is a protocol for connecting different ledgers, including blockchain and non-blockchain ledgers. It enables the seamless transfer of value between different payment networks, making it possible to send and receive payments across different currencies and payment systems. The ILP is an open protocol, which means that anyone can use it to connect different payment networks and create new payment applications.

Ripple has also developed a range of software solutions that enable financial institutions and payment providers to integrate with the Ripple ecosystem. These solutions include xCurrent, which enables real-time messaging and settlement between financial institutions, and xRapid, which uses XRP as a bridge currency to facilitate cross-border payments.

One of the key benefits of the Ripple ecosystem is that it is designed to be interoperable with other payment networks and systems. This means that financial institutions and payment providers can easily integrate with the Ripple ecosystem without having to replace their existing payment systems. This interoperability also enables the seamless transfer of value between different payment networks, reducing the cost and complexity of cross-border payments.

Another important aspect of the Ripple ecosystem is the Ripple community. The Ripple community consists of developers, entrepreneurs, investors, and other stakeholders who are passionate about the development and adoption of Ripple and XRP. The community has played a vital role in the development of the Ripple ecosystem, contributing to the development of new applications, tools, and services that enable the adoption of Ripple and XRP.

In conclusion, the development of the Ripple ecosystem has been a key factor in the success of Ripple and XRP. The Ripple ecosystem consists of various components, including RippleNet, the XRP Ledger, and the Interledger Protocol, as well as a range of software solutions and a passionate community of stakeholders. These components work together to facilitate cross-border payments and enable the adoption of Ripple and XRP, improving the overall efficiency of the global payments system.

The impact of the community on Ripple's roadmap

The Ripple community, which includes developers, investors, and users, has played an important role in shaping Ripple's technology and future roadmap. In this section, we will explore how the Ripple community has influenced the company's direction and the impact it has had on the development of Ripple's technology.

Open Source Development

One of the most notable ways the Ripple community has impacted the company's technology is through open-source development. Ripple has always been committed to open-source development, but the company's engagement with the community has become more formalized in recent years.

The company has established RippleNet Accelerator Program to encourage developers to create new applications on top of Ripple's technology. Through this program, Ripple offers financial support, technical resources, and mentorship to developers who want to build new applications using Ripple's technology.

This program has helped to foster a growing ecosystem of developers who are building innovative applications on top of Ripple's technology. Ripple has also partnered with various open-source communities to collaborate on the development of its technology. For example, Ripple has partnered with the Linux Foundation to develop the Interledger Protocol (ILP), an open-source protocol that enables interoperability between different payment networks.

Community Feedback

Another way the Ripple community has influenced the company's direction is through feedback. Ripple is known for actively engaging with its community, and the company is always looking for ways to improve its technology and services. Ripple has a number of channels through which community members can provide feedback, including forums, social media, and the RippleX community platform.

Ripple has shown a willingness to take community feedback into account when making decisions about its technology and services. For example, in 2019, Ripple announced that it would be shifting its focus away from XRP sales to focus more on product development. This decision was made in response to feedback from the community, which had expressed concern that Ripple's XRP sales were having a negative impact on the cryptocurrency's price.

Community Events

The Ripple community has also played a key role in organizing events and meetups to promote Ripple's technology and bring community members together. These events provide an opportunity for community members to learn more about Ripple's technology, share ideas, and network with other members of the community.

Ripple has also sponsored a number of events and conferences focused on blockchain and fintech, such as the Blockchain Summit and the Money 20/20 conference. These events provide Ripple with an opportunity to showcase its technology and engage with potential partners and customers.

Impact on Ripple's Roadmap

The Ripple community has had a significant impact on Ripple's roadmap, particularly in terms of the company's focus on developing new products and services. Ripple has always been committed to building technology that solves real-world problems, and the company's engagement with the community has helped it to identify key areas where its technology can make a difference.

For example, in 2020, Ripple announced the launch of On-Demand Liquidity (ODL), a product that enables instant cross-border payments using XRP. This product was developed in response to feedback from the community, which had identified the need for a faster and more efficient cross-border payment solution.

In addition to ODL, Ripple has also developed a number of other products and services based on feedback from the community. For example, Ripple's Payburner wallet developed in response to feedback from community members who wanted a more user-friendly and secure way to store and use XRP.

Conclusion

The Ripple community has played a vital role in shaping the company's technology and future roadmap. Through open-source development, feedback, events, and engagement with the RippleX community platform, the Ripple community has helped to foster a growing ecosystem of developers and users who are building innovative applications on top of Ripple's technology. The impact of the community on Ripple's roadmap has been significant, with the

Future prospects for the Ripple community

As the Ripple ecosystem continues to evolve and grow, so too does the Ripple community. The community has been instrumental in Ripple's success, and its role is expected to become even more important in the future. In this section, we will explore the future prospects for the Ripple community, including its potential impact on Ripple's development and adoption.

One of the most important future prospects for the Ripple community is its ability to drive adoption of Ripple's products and services. The community has been a powerful force in spreading awareness of Ripple and XRP, and this is likely to continue in the future. By advocating for Ripple and XRP and demonstrating their benefits to potential users, the community can help to drive adoption of these technologies.

Another important future prospect for the Ripple community is its potential to shape the development of the Ripple ecosystem. As Ripple continues to expand and develop new products and services, the community can play an important role in providing feedback and guidance to Ripple's development team. This feedback can help to ensure that Ripple's products and services are tailored to meet the needs of the community and the wider market.

In addition, the community can also play a key role in shaping the regulatory environment for Ripple and XRP. As governments and regulatory bodies around the world grapple with the challenges of regulating cryptocurrencies, the Ripple community can provide valuable input and guidance on how best to approach these issues. By working closely with regulators and other stakeholders, the community can help to create a regulatory environment that supports the growth and adoption of Ripple and XRP.

One potential challenge for the Ripple community in the future is the need to balance the interests of different stakeholders. As Ripple continues to grow and evolve, there may be competing interests within the community, including the interests of investors, developers, users, and other stakeholders. The community will need to find ways to balance these interests and work together towards a shared vision for the future of Ripple and XRP.

Another challenge for the Ripple community is the need to maintain its collaborative and decentralized culture as the ecosystem continues to grow. The community has been successful in fostering a culture of collaboration and cooperation, which has been instrumental in Ripple's success. As the ecosystem continues to expand, however, it may become more difficult to maintain this culture. The community will need to find ways to ensure that it remains open and inclusive, while also maintaining a sense of shared purpose and direction.

Despite these challenges, the future prospects for the Ripple community are bright. As Ripple continues to grow and evolve, the community is likely to play an increasingly important role in driving adoption, shaping the development of the ecosystem, and creating a regulatory environment that supports the growth and adoption of Ripple and XRP. By working together and maintaining a collaborative culture, the community can help to ensure that Ripple and XRP continue to thrive in the years to come.

Chapter 6: The Regulation of Ripple and XRP
Overview of the regulatory landscape for Ripple and XRP

Ripple and XRP have garnered significant attention from regulatory bodies worldwide due to their potential impact on the financial industry. As a result, regulatory bodies have taken a keen interest in understanding how Ripple and XRP operate and how they may fit within the existing regulatory framework. This section will provide an overview of the regulatory landscape for Ripple and XRP and how different regulatory bodies around the world view these digital assets.

Regulatory Landscape in the United States

In the United States, the regulatory landscape for Ripple and XRP is complex and has undergone significant changes in recent years. The US Securities and Exchange Commission (SEC) has taken a particularly keen interest in Ripple and XRP, as it has argued that the sale of XRP should be considered an unregistered securities offering. The SEC filed a lawsuit against Ripple Labs in December 2020, alleging that Ripple had raised $1.3 billion through an unregistered securities offering. Ripple has denied these allegations and has vowed to fight the lawsuit.

The outcome of the lawsuit will have significant implications for the regulatory status of XRP in the United States. If the court determines that XRP is a security, it would need to be registered with the SEC, which could have a significant impact on the asset's liquidity and trading volume.

On the other hand, if the court determines that XRP is not a security, it would likely be subject to regulation as a commodity, which would have a less significant impact on its trading.

Regulatory Landscape in Europe

In Europe, regulatory bodies have taken a more nuanced approach to Ripple and XRP. The European Securities and Markets Authority (ESMA) has issued guidance that suggests that XRP may be classified as a security under certain circumstances. However, this guidance is not binding, and each member state of the European Union has its own regulatory regime for cryptocurrencies. Some countries, such as Switzerland, have taken a more favorable approach to Ripple and XRP, with the Swiss Financial Market Supervisory Authority (FINMA) classifying XRP as a "payment token" rather than a security.

Regulatory Landscape in Asia

In Asia, the regulatory landscape for Ripple and XRP is also varied. Japan, which is home to one of the largest cryptocurrency markets in the world, has taken a relatively favorable approach to Ripple and XRP. The Japanese Financial Services Agency (FSA) has classified XRP as a cryptocurrency, which means that it is subject to regulation under Japan's Payment Services Act.

China, on the other hand, has taken a more restrictive approach to cryptocurrencies, and Ripple and XRP are not currently available for trading on Chinese exchanges. However, it is worth noting that China has been experimenting with a central bank digital currency (CBDC), which could have significant implications for the cryptocurrency market in the future.

Implications of Regulation on Ripple and XRP

The regulatory landscape for Ripple and XRP is complex, and the regulatory status of these assets can vary significantly depending on the jurisdiction. This complexity can make it challenging for financial institutions and investors to navigate the market for Ripple and XRP.

In addition, regulatory uncertainty can also have an impact on the price and liquidity of Ripple and XRP. If a regulatory body were to classify XRP as a security, for example, it could significantly impact the asset's trading volume and liquidity. This uncertainty has led some financial institutions to take a cautious approach to Ripple and XRP, while others have embraced the potential benefits of these digital assets despite the regulatory uncertainty.

Overall, the regulatory landscape for Ripple and XRP is likely to continue to evolve in the coming years, and it will be essential for investors and financial institutions to stay up-to-date with these changes to ensure they are making informed decisions about the use of these assets.

The SEC lawsuit against Ripple and XRP

The SEC lawsuit against Ripple and XRP is a significant event that has garnered attention from the cryptocurrency community and the financial industry. In this section, we will discuss the background of the lawsuit, the allegations made by the SEC, and Ripple's response.

Background

In December 2020, the US Securities and Exchange Commission (SEC) filed a lawsuit against Ripple Labs Inc. and two of its executives, Chris Larsen and Brad Garlinghouse. The lawsuit alleged that Ripple raised $1.3 billion through an unregistered securities offering of XRP tokens. The SEC claimed that Ripple had been selling XRP tokens as an investment contract, which is a security under US law.

Allegations by the SEC

The SEC's complaint against Ripple claimed that Ripple and its executives engaged in an ongoing illegal securities offering since 2013. The SEC argued that Ripple sold XRP tokens to investors with the promise that the tokens would increase in value. The SEC also claimed that Ripple used the proceeds from the sales to fund its operations, and the company's executives sold XRP tokens while they knew that the tokens were unregistered securities.

The SEC's allegations were based on the Howey test, which is a legal test used to determine whether an instrument is a security. According to the Howey test, an instrument is considered a security if it involves an investment of money in a common enterprise with the expectation of profits solely from the efforts of others.

Ripple's response

In response to the SEC lawsuit, Ripple denied the allegations and claimed that XRP was not a security. Ripple argued that XRP was a currency used to facilitate international transactions and that the company had no control over the value of the tokens. Ripple also claimed that the SEC had not provided clear guidance on whether XRP was a security, making it difficult for the company to comply with the law.

Ripple's legal team also argued that the SEC had taken a selective approach to enforcement, as other cryptocurrencies had been sold without registering as securities, and the SEC had not taken action against them.

Impact on Ripple and XRP

The SEC lawsuit has had a significant impact on Ripple and XRP. After the lawsuit was filed, several cryptocurrency exchanges suspended trading in XRP, citing the regulatory uncertainty. XRP's price also dropped significantly, losing more than 70% of its value.

The lawsuit has also raised concerns among the cryptocurrency community about the regulatory status of other cryptocurrencies. Many industry experts have argued that the lack of clear guidance from regulators has created uncertainty, making it difficult for companies to comply with the law.

Future prospects

The outcome of the SEC lawsuit against Ripple and XRP is uncertain, and it is unclear how it will impact the regulatory status of other cryptocurrencies. However, the lawsuit has highlighted the need for clear guidance from regulators, which could help prevent future legal disputes.

Many in the cryptocurrency community have called for a regulatory framework that provides clarity for companies and investors. The framework should also balance the need to protect investors while promoting innovation in the industry. Some regulators have started taking steps to provide clear guidelines. For example, in 2020, the Office of the Comptroller of the Currency (OCC) issued guidance allowing banks to provide cryptocurrency custody services.

Updated Situation

The current situation of the SEC lawsuit against Ripple and XRP up to Jan 2023 is that both parties are waiting for a decision from the court after submitting their final filings. The SEC claims that Ripple sold unregistered securities in the form of XRP tokens, while Ripple denies this and argues that XRP is a digital currency, not a security. The outcome of the case could have significant implications for the future of XRP and other cryptocurrencies.

In conclusion, the SEC lawsuit against Ripple and XRP is a significant event that has raised questions about the regulatory status of cryptocurrencies. While the outcome of the lawsuit is uncertain, it has highlighted the need for clear guidance from regulators to promote innovation in the industry while protecting investors.

The implications of the SEC lawsuit for Ripple and XRP

The SEC lawsuit against Ripple and XRP has far-reaching implications for both the company and the cryptocurrency industry as a whole. In this section, we will examine the potential impact of the lawsuit on Ripple and XRP, as well as the broader implications for the regulation of cryptocurrencies.

First, let's review the main allegations of the lawsuit. The SEC claims that Ripple and its executives sold XRP as an unregistered security, violating US securities laws. The SEC argues that XRP meets the definition of an investment contract, as outlined in the Howey Test, and therefore should have been registered as a security with the SEC before being sold to investors.

Ripple has vigorously contested the allegations, arguing that XRP is not a security but a currency or a digital asset. Ripple maintains that XRP was created to be a medium of exchange and a bridge currency for cross-border payments, and that it is not an investment contract because it does not represent an ownership interest in Ripple or provide holders with a share of Ripple's profits.

So what are the implications of the lawsuit for Ripple and XRP? The most immediate consequence is that it has caused a significant drop in the value of XRP. After the SEC announced the lawsuit in December 2020, the price of XRP plummeted from around $0.60 to $0.20, and it has struggled to recover since. This has had a ripple effect (no pun intended) on Ripple's business, as it has made it harder for Ripple to convince financial institutions to adopt its technology and use XRP in their payment flows.

The lawsuit has also forced Ripple to divert resources away from its growth initiatives and focus on defending itself in court. Ripple has incurred substantial legal costs and has had to put some of its partnerships on hold as it waits for the lawsuit to be resolved.

Another potential consequence of the lawsuit is that it could set a precedent for how cryptocurrencies are regulated in the US. If the court sides with the SEC and finds that XRP is a security, it could have implications for other cryptocurrencies that were sold in a similar manner. This could result in a regulatory crackdown on the entire cryptocurrency industry, leading to increased scrutiny and compliance costs for cryptocurrency companies.

On the other hand, if the court rules in favor of Ripple and finds that XRP is not a security, it could provide clarity and certainty for the industry and pave the way for more widespread adoption of cryptocurrencies by mainstream financial institutions. It could also serve as a model for how to properly structure and market cryptocurrency offerings in a way that complies with securities laws.

Regardless of the outcome, the SEC lawsuit has highlighted the need for clearer regulations around cryptocurrencies. The lack of regulatory clarity has been a major impediment to the adoption of cryptocurrencies by mainstream financial institutions and has contributed to the perception that cryptocurrencies are risky and unreliable.

In response to the lawsuit, several US lawmakers have called for clearer regulations for cryptocurrencies. In December 2020, Representative Tom Emmer introduced a bill called the Securities Clarity Act, which aims to provide a clear definition of securities and exempt digital tokens that meet certain criteria from securities laws.

In conclusion, the SEC lawsuit against Ripple and XRP has significant implications for both the company and the cryptocurrency industry as a whole. The outcome of the lawsuit could set a precedent for how cryptocurrencies are regulated in the US and could either provide clarity and certainty for the industry or result in increased regulatory scrutiny and compliance costs. Regardless of the outcome, the lawsuit has highlighted the need for clearer regulations around cryptocurrencies and may spur lawmakers to take action to provide greater regulatory clarity.

The response of Ripple and XRP to the lawsuit

The lawsuit filed by the U.S. Securities and Exchange Commission (SEC) against Ripple Labs and its executives in December 2020 has been one of the most significant legal challenges facing the cryptocurrency industry in recent times. Ripple and its affiliated digital asset XRP were accused of conducting an unregistered securities offering worth over $1.3 billion.

Ripple has since then publicly denied the SEC's allegations and defended its stance, stating that XRP is a digital currency rather than a security. In this section, we will delve deeper into Ripple's response to the lawsuit and examine the key arguments put forth by the company and its legal team.

Ripple's initial response to the lawsuit was robust. The company's CEO, Brad Garlinghouse, took to Twitter to defend the company and criticized the SEC for its handling of the case. Garlinghouse argued that the SEC's action against Ripple would harm innovation and technological advancement in the United States. He also asserted that Ripple would fight the lawsuit vigorously and urged other cryptocurrency companies to join forces in the fight against regulatory overreach.

Ripple also released an official statement denying the SEC's allegations and highlighting its commitment to complying with all applicable laws and regulations. The statement asserted that XRP is a digital currency and not a security, and therefore not subject to SEC regulation. Ripple also emphasized that XRP's status as a digital currency had been recognized by several other regulatory bodies worldwide, including the Financial Conduct Authority (FCA) in the UK.

In February 2021, Ripple filed a formal response to the SEC's lawsuit, which challenged the SEC's jurisdiction over XRP and Ripple. Ripple's response asserted that XRP was a currency and not a security and therefore fell outside the SEC's regulatory purview. Ripple also argued that the SEC had not given fair notice to market participants regarding its position on XRP's regulatory status, and therefore any enforcement action against Ripple would be unconstitutional.

Ripple also argued that the SEC's lawsuit had caused significant harm to XRP holders, who had suffered substantial losses in the wake of the SEC's allegations. Ripple claimed that the SEC's action had caused a "massive disruption" to the XRP market and that its legal action had caused "irreparable harm" to Ripple's reputation.

The case has since then entered the discovery phase, with both sides requesting access to relevant documents and evidence. Ripple has also filed several motions to dismiss the lawsuit, citing various legal and procedural grounds.

The outcome of the SEC lawsuit will have significant implications for Ripple, XRP, and the wider cryptocurrency industry. If the SEC's allegations are upheld, it could potentially lead to significant penalties for Ripple and could result in XRP being classified as a security, subject to strict regulatory oversight.

On the other hand, if Ripple's arguments prevail, it could potentially set a precedent for other cryptocurrency companies, providing greater clarity regarding the regulatory status of digital assets.

In conclusion, Ripple's response to the SEC lawsuit has been robust, with the company defending its position on XRP's status as a digital currency. The outcome of the lawsuit will be keenly watched by the cryptocurrency industry and could have significant implications for the regulatory landscape of digital assets.

Future prospects for the regulation of Ripple and XRP

The regulatory landscape for cryptocurrencies and blockchain technology is still evolving, and Ripple and XRP are no exception. The SEC lawsuit against Ripple has raised questions about the status of XRP as a security and the future of Ripple's business model. In this section, we will examine the potential future regulatory developments and their impact on Ripple and XRP.

Regulatory Clarity

One of the key challenges facing Ripple and XRP is regulatory clarity. There is still considerable uncertainty around how cryptocurrencies should be regulated, with different countries taking different approaches. Some countries have embraced cryptocurrencies, while others have banned them outright. This lack of clarity has led to a patchwork of regulations that can be difficult for companies like Ripple to navigate.

However, there are some signs that regulatory clarity may be improving. In the United States, the SEC has indicated that it is open to working with companies in the cryptocurrency industry to help them comply with regulations. Additionally, the Biden administration has appointed a number of officials with experience in the cryptocurrency industry, which suggests that the government may take a more favorable view of cryptocurrencies going forward.

Classification as a Security

The SEC lawsuit against Ripple has raised questions about whether XRP should be classified as a security. If XRP is classified as a security, it would be subject to a much more stringent regulatory framework than it is currently. This could have a significant impact on Ripple's business model and the future of XRP.

However, there is still some uncertainty around whether XRP should be classified as a security. Ripple has argued that XRP is not a security, but rather a currency that is used to facilitate international payments. Some experts have also suggested that XRP does not meet the criteria for a security, as it does not represent an ownership stake in a company and is not sold as an investment.

It remains to be seen how the SEC lawsuit will be resolved and what impact it will have on the classification of XRP. However, if XRP is ultimately classified as a security, it could have a significant impact on Ripple's business model and the future of the cryptocurrency.

Anti-Money Laundering Regulations

Anti-money laundering (AML) regulations are another area where Ripple and XRP are likely to face increased scrutiny. The use of cryptocurrencies for illicit purposes has been a concern for regulators for some time, and AML regulations are designed to prevent money laundering and other illegal activities.

Ripple has been proactive in addressing these concerns, and has implemented a number of measures to prevent the use of XRP for illegal activities. For example, Ripple has developed a system for tracking XRP transactions and has partnered with a number of blockchain analysis firms to identify potential criminal activity.

However, as the regulatory landscape continues to evolve, it is likely that AML regulations will become more stringent. This could create additional challenges for Ripple and XRP, and may require the development of new compliance systems and procedures.

Conclusion

The regulatory landscape for cryptocurrencies and blockchain technology is still evolving, and Ripple and XRP are likely to face continued scrutiny from regulators in the coming years. However, there are also signs that regulatory clarity may be improving, and that governments may take a more favorable view of cryptocurrencies in the future.

The outcome of the SEC lawsuit against Ripple is likely to have a significant impact on the future of XRP and Ripple's business model. If XRP is ultimately classified as a security, it could lead to a more stringent regulatory framework that could make it more difficult for Ripple to operate.

Despite these challenges, Ripple has shown a commitment to compliance and has been proactive in addressing regulatory concerns. The company has also been actively working to develop new use cases for XRP and to expand the Ripple ecosystem.

Looking forward, the regulation of Ripple and XRP is likely to become more complex and nuanced as the cryptocurrency industry continues to evolve. As more governments and financial institutions around the world explore the use of blockchain technology and digital assets, there will be a growing need for clear and consistent regulations that can support innovation while also protecting consumers and maintaining financial stability.

One potential avenue for further regulation of Ripple and XRP could be through the development of global regulatory frameworks. The Financial Action Task Force (FATF), an intergovernmental organization that sets international standards for anti-money laundering and counter-terrorism financing, has already issued guidance on the regulation of virtual assets and has called on countries to adopt a risk-based approach to regulating the cryptocurrency industry.

Another potential development in the regulation of Ripple and XRP could be the emergence of new forms of regulation that are specifically tailored to digital assets. For example, some experts have suggested that digital assets could be regulated under a new category of financial instrument, such as a "crypto security" or "digital asset security." This could provide a clearer regulatory framework for digital assets that are used as investment vehicles, while also recognizing the unique characteristics of these assets.

In conclusion, the regulation of Ripple and XRP will continue to be a complex and evolving issue in the cryptocurrency industry. While the SEC lawsuit has raised significant challenges for Ripple and XRP, the company has shown a commitment to compliance and has been actively working to address regulatory concerns. Looking forward, the development of global regulatory frameworks and the emergence of new forms of regulation could help to provide clearer and more consistent rules for the cryptocurrency industry, which could ultimately benefit Ripple and XRP as well as the wider ecosystem.

Chapter 7: The Potential of Ripple and XRP
The untapped potential of Ripple and XRP

As one of the pioneers in the world of blockchain and cryptocurrency, Ripple and its associated digital asset XRP have been at the forefront of the movement towards faster, cheaper, and more efficient cross-border payments. While the technology has already made significant inroads in this area, there is still much untapped potential for Ripple and XRP to revolutionize the way that we conduct financial transactions.

One area where Ripple and XRP have the potential to make a major impact is in the remittance market. According to the World Bank, remittances to low- and middle-income countries reached a record high of $540 billion in 2020, despite the challenges posed by the COVID-19 pandemic. However, many of these transactions still involve high fees and lengthy processing times, particularly for smaller transactions. By leveraging the speed and efficiency of blockchain technology, Ripple and XRP could dramatically reduce the cost and time required to send money across borders, making it easier for people around the world to access the financial services they need.

Another area where Ripple and XRP could make a major impact is in the world of micropayments. Currently, it is often not cost-effective to process small transactions due to the high fees charged by traditional payment processors. However, with Ripple and XRP, transactions can be processed quickly and cheaply, making it possible to send and receive even the smallest amounts of money. This has the potential to unlock a whole new world of possibilities for online transactions, particularly in developing countries where access to traditional banking services may be limited.

In addition to these use cases, Ripple and XRP also have the potential to revolutionize the way that financial institutions interact with one another. By using the Ripple network and XRP, banks and other financial institutions can settle transactions in real-time, without the need for intermediaries or lengthy processing times. This has the potential to reduce the risk of fraud and errors, while also improving the speed and efficiency of the financial system as a whole.

Of course, there are still many challenges that must be overcome before Ripple and XRP can fully realize their potential. In addition to regulatory hurdles, there are also technical challenges to be addressed, such as scalability and interoperability with other blockchain platforms. However, with a strong community of supporters and a commitment to innovation and development, Ripple and XRP are well-positioned to continue making strides in these areas.

Ultimately, the untapped potential of Ripple and XRP lies in their ability to democratize access to financial services and reduce the cost and time required to conduct transactions. By leveraging the power of blockchain technology, Ripple and XRP have the potential to make a real difference in the lives of people around the world, particularly those in developing countries who may currently lack access to affordable and efficient financial services.

The use cases of Ripple and XRP beyond cross-border payments

Ripple and its native digital currency XRP have gained significant attention and adoption in the cross-border payment industry. However, the potential use cases for Ripple and XRP extend far beyond just cross-border payments. In this section, we will explore some of the other potential use cases for Ripple and XRP.

Global Money Transfers: Ripple and XRP can be used for global money transfers, not just for cross-border payments. For instance, the platform can be used by individuals and businesses to send money to family members, friends, or business partners around the world. Ripple's low transaction fees and fast transaction times make it an attractive option for global money transfers.

Supply Chain Management: Ripple's technology can also be used in supply chain management. The platform can be used to track goods and ensure that they are shipped from the manufacturer to the retailer securely and efficiently. Ripple's blockchain technology can also be used to verify the authenticity of goods, thereby reducing the risk of fraud and counterfeiting.

Real Estate Transactions: The real estate industry can also benefit from Ripple and XRP's technology. The platform can be used to facilitate real estate transactions, making the process faster and more secure. Ripple's blockchain technology can be used to verify the authenticity of property titles and streamline the transfer of ownership.

Micropayments: Ripple's low transaction fees and fast transaction times make it an attractive option for micropayments. The platform can be used to facilitate small transactions, such as paying for online content, gaming, and in-app purchases.

Decentralized Finance (DeFi): The rise of decentralized finance (DeFi) has brought new opportunities for Ripple and XRP. The platform can be used to facilitate DeFi transactions, such as borrowing and lending, trading, and staking. Ripple's blockchain technology can also be used to create new financial products and services, such as insurance and investment products.

Gaming: Ripple and XRP can also be used in the gaming industry. The platform can be used to facilitate in-game purchases and transactions, making the process faster and more secure. Ripple's blockchain technology can also be used to verify the authenticity of in-game assets, reducing the risk of fraud and counterfeiting.

Identity Verification: Ripple's blockchain technology can be used to verify the authenticity of identity documents, such as passports and driver's licenses. This can help reduce the risk of identity theft and fraud, and provide a more secure and efficient way of verifying identities.

Overall, the potential use cases for Ripple and XRP are vast and varied. While the platform has gained significant adoption in the cross-border payment industry, its technology can be applied to a wide range of industries and use cases. As the platform continues to evolve and grow, it will be interesting to see how these potential use cases are developed and adopted.

The potential impact of Ripple and XRP on the financial industry

The financial industry is undergoing a transformation as new technologies, such as blockchain and cryptocurrencies, are disrupting traditional business models. Ripple and XRP are well-positioned to be at the forefront of this disruption, with the potential to transform the financial industry in a number of ways.

One of the most significant potential impacts of Ripple and XRP is in the area of cross-border payments, which we have discussed extensively in previous chapters. By enabling faster and cheaper cross-border payments, Ripple and XRP could significantly reduce the costs and time involved in international money transfers. This could have a significant impact on the global economy, enabling businesses and individuals to more easily engage in international trade and commerce.

Beyond cross-border payments, Ripple and XRP have the potential to impact a range of other financial services, including remittances, micropayments, and peer-to-peer payments. For example, Ripple's xRapid solution could be used for remittances, enabling faster and cheaper transfers of funds between countries. Meanwhile, XRP could be used for micropayments and peer-to-peer payments, enabling users to make small transactions quickly and easily.

Another area where Ripple and XRP could have a significant impact is in the world of digital assets. With the rise of cryptocurrencies, there is a growing need for infrastructure to support the trading and exchange of these assets. Ripple and XRP could provide this infrastructure, enabling faster and more secure transactions of digital assets. This could also enable the creation of new financial products and services, such as tokenized securities, that are built on top of the Ripple network.

Ripple and XRP could also have a significant impact on the world of banking. As we have discussed, Ripple's solutions are designed to work within the existing banking system, enabling banks to offer faster and cheaper cross-border payments to their customers. This could make banks more competitive in the global marketplace, and could help to reduce the costs associated with international money transfers.

In addition, Ripple and XRP could help to increase financial inclusion, particularly in developing countries where access to traditional banking services is limited. By enabling faster and cheaper cross-border payments and other financial services, Ripple and XRP could help to bring more people into the formal financial system, providing them with access to credit, savings, and other financial services.

Overall, the potential impact of Ripple and XRP on the financial industry is significant. By enabling faster, cheaper, and more secure transactions, Ripple and XRP could transform the way we think about money and finance. However, it is important to note that there are still challenges and obstacles to overcome, including regulatory hurdles and competition from other blockchain and cryptocurrency projects. Nevertheless, the potential rewards of success are substantial, and Ripple and XRP are well-positioned to play a major role in the future of finance.

The role of Ripple and XRP in the future of money

As the financial industry undergoes rapid change, many experts are predicting that digital assets will play a significant role in the future of money. Ripple and XRP are at the forefront of this trend, offering a faster, cheaper, and more efficient way to move money around the world. In this section, we will explore the potential role of Ripple and XRP in the future of money.

The shift to digital currencies:

As consumers become more comfortable with digital payments, there is a growing shift towards digital currencies. This trend is likely to continue as more countries explore the creation of central bank digital currencies (CBDCs). Ripple and XRP are well-positioned to benefit from this trend, as they offer a fast and efficient way to move digital currencies around the world.

The rise of decentralized finance:

Decentralized finance (DeFi) is a growing trend in the financial industry, offering a new way to access financial services without the need for traditional banks. Ripple and XRP have the potential to play a significant role in the development of DeFi, offering a fast and efficient way to move digital assets between different DeFi platforms.

The impact on traditional banking:

As digital currencies become more prevalent, traditional banks may struggle to keep up with the pace of change. Ripple and XRP offer an alternative to traditional banking, allowing customers to move money quickly and easily without the need for a bank account. This could have a significant impact on the traditional banking industry, with many experts predicting a decline in the use of traditional banks in the future.

The potential for financial inclusion:

One of the most significant benefits of digital currencies is the potential for financial inclusion. By offering a fast and efficient way to move money around the world, Ripple and XRP have the potential to bring financial services to people who were previously excluded from the traditional banking system. This could have a significant impact on developing countries, where many people do not have access to basic financial services.

The impact on cross-border payments:

Cross-border payments are a significant pain point in the traditional banking system, with many transactions taking several days to complete and incurring high fees. Ripple and XRP offer a fast and efficient way to move money across borders, with transactions typically settling in a matter of seconds. This could have a significant impact on the global economy, allowing businesses to move money quickly and easily across borders.

The potential for innovation:

As digital currencies continue to evolve, there is a significant potential for innovation in the financial industry.

Ripple and XRP are at the forefront of this trend, offering a new way to move money around the world. As more companies explore the potential of digital currencies, we are likely to see significant innovation in the financial industry in the coming years.

Conclusion:

Ripple and XRP have the potential to play a significant role in the future of money. As the financial industry undergoes rapid change, digital currencies are likely to become increasingly important. Ripple and XRP offer a fast, efficient, and cost-effective way to move money around the world, with significant potential for financial inclusion, innovation, and disruption of the traditional banking industry. While there are still many challenges to overcome, the future looks bright for Ripple and XRP.

Future prospects for Ripple and XRP's potential

As Ripple and XRP continue to develop and expand their use cases, the potential for these technologies to transform the financial industry remains significant. However, several factors could impact the future prospects of Ripple and XRP's potential.

One of the main factors that could impact Ripple and XRP's potential is regulatory uncertainty. The ongoing SEC lawsuit against Ripple has highlighted the need for clear regulatory guidance around digital assets. Until there is greater regulatory clarity, financial institutions may be hesitant to fully adopt Ripple and XRP's technologies.

Another factor that could impact Ripple and XRP's potential is competition. While Ripple has already established itself as a leader in cross-border payments, other blockchain-based companies are developing similar solutions. These competitors could potentially eat into Ripple's market share and limit the potential growth of Ripple and XRP.

However, Ripple has several advantages that could help it maintain its leadership position in the industry. For example, the company has a robust ecosystem that includes partnerships with more than 300 financial institutions. These partnerships provide Ripple with a strong network effect, making it more difficult for competitors to gain traction in the market.

Ripple's strong financial position is another advantage that could help it succeed in the long term. Unlike many other blockchain startups, Ripple has significant financial resources, having raised over $94 million in funding. This financial stability allows Ripple to invest in research and development, build new partnerships, and expand its ecosystem.

Another factor that could impact Ripple and XRP's potential is the broader adoption of blockchain technology. As more financial institutions adopt blockchain-based solutions, the demand for Ripple and XRP's technologies could increase. Additionally, the development of new use cases for blockchain technology could open up new opportunities for Ripple and XRP.

Overall, the future prospects for Ripple and XRP's potential are promising, but there are several challenges that the company will need to navigate. As regulatory uncertainty continues to be a concern, Ripple will need to work closely with regulators to ensure that its technologies are compliant with applicable laws and regulations. Additionally, as competition increases, Ripple will need to continue to innovate and differentiate itself in the market.

However, Ripple has already demonstrated its ability to succeed in the highly competitive fintech industry. With a strong ecosystem, significant financial resources, and a commitment to innovation, Ripple and XRP are well-positioned to continue transforming the financial industry for years to come. As blockchain technology becomes more widespread,

Ripple and XRP's potential impact on the future of money could be even greater than previously anticipated.

Ripple and XRP have been subject to various criticisms from within the cryptocurrency community and beyond. Some of the main criticisms of Ripple and XRP include:

Centralization: One of the main criticisms of Ripple is its level of centralization. Unlike other decentralized cryptocurrencies, Ripple is run by a centralized company, Ripple Labs, which has control over the development and governance of the Ripple network. This has led to concerns about the potential for censorship and control by a single entity.

Pre-mined tokens: XRP was created with 100 billion tokens in existence, of which 80 billion were held by Ripple Labs. This has led to criticism that XRP is not truly decentralized, as the majority of the tokens are held by a single entity.

Lack of adoption: Despite Ripple's efforts to promote XRP as a bridge currency for cross-border payments, adoption of the cryptocurrency by financial institutions has been slow. This has led some to question the viability of Ripple's business model.

Security concerns: There have been concerns raised about the security of the Ripple network, with some experts suggesting that the consensus algorithm used by the network may be vulnerable to attacks.

Regulatory risks: As discussed in Chapter 6, Ripple and XRP are subject to regulatory risks, particularly in relation to the SEC's lawsuit against Ripple. Some critics argue that the regulatory risks associated with Ripple and XRP make them less attractive as investments.

Lack of transparency: Some critics have raised concerns about the lack of transparency around Ripple's operations, particularly in relation to its sales of XRP tokens.

Despite these criticisms, Ripple and XRP have continued to attract interest from investors and financial institutions. In the following sections, we will explore these criticisms in more detail and discuss Ripple's response to them.

The centralization of Ripple and XRP

One of the most significant criticisms of Ripple and XRP is their level of centralization. Unlike decentralized cryptocurrencies like Bitcoin and Ethereum, Ripple and XRP have a more centralized structure, which has led to concerns over their long-term viability and sustainability. In this section, we will explore the centralization of Ripple and XRP, the criticisms surrounding it, and the potential implications for the future of the technology.

Centralization of Ripple:

Ripple's centralization is primarily attributed to the company's control over the XRP ledger, the underlying technology that powers XRP. Unlike decentralized cryptocurrencies, the XRP ledger is maintained by a select group of nodes that are primarily controlled by Ripple. This means that Ripple has a significant amount of control over the network's decision-making process, making it more centralized than other cryptocurrencies.

The centralization of Ripple has led to criticisms from the cryptocurrency community, which often values decentralization as a core tenet of the technology. Critics argue that Ripple's centralization makes it more susceptible to censorship, manipulation, and government intervention, which undermines the principles of decentralization that cryptocurrencies are built on.

Centralization of XRP:

Another aspect of Ripple's centralization is the distribution of XRP tokens. Unlike Bitcoin, which is mined by a network of decentralized nodes, XRP was initially pre-mined by Ripple, and a significant portion of the tokens are still held by the company. This means that Ripple has control over a significant portion of the XRP supply, which could be used to influence the market's value.

Critics of XRP's centralization argue that this distribution model goes against the decentralized nature of cryptocurrencies and could be used to manipulate the market's value. Furthermore, the fact that Ripple holds such a large portion of the token supply raises concerns about the company's ability to influence the XRP market's direction and could lead to conflicts of interest between Ripple and XRP holders.

Potential Implications:

The centralization of Ripple and XRP raises several concerns about the technology's long-term viability and sustainability. Critics argue that Ripple's centralization makes it more susceptible to government intervention and regulation, which could undermine the technology's core principles. Furthermore, the centralization of XRP's distribution model raises concerns about the token's value and potential manipulation of the market.

However, proponents of Ripple and XRP argue that the technology's centralization is necessary to achieve the level of scalability and transaction speed required to compete with traditional payment systems. Furthermore, Ripple has shown a commitment to compliance and has been working to address regulatory concerns, which could help alleviate concerns over government intervention.

Conclusion:

The centralization of Ripple and XRP remains a significant concern for critics of the technology. The fact that Ripple has a significant amount of control over the XRP ledger and distribution model raises concerns about the technology's long-term viability and sustainability. However, proponents argue that the technology's centralization is necessary to achieve the level of scalability and transaction speed required to compete with traditional payment systems.

Ultimately, the future of Ripple and XRP will depend on how well the company can address these concerns and balance the need for centralization with the principles of decentralization that underpin the cryptocurrency industry. As the technology continues to evolve and mature, it will be interesting to see how Ripple and XRP navigate these challenges and continue to innovate in the world of payments and finance.

The privacy concerns surrounding Ripple and XRP

Ripple and XRP have faced criticism over privacy concerns due to the nature of their technology and the way it operates. While the Ripple network and XRP are designed to be fast, efficient, and transparent, this transparency has also led to concerns around user privacy and security.

One of the key concerns around Ripple and XRP is the fact that transactions are publicly visible on the blockchain. This means that anyone can see the details of transactions, including the sender and recipient's addresses, as well as the amount and time of the transaction. While this level of transparency can be beneficial in some cases, such as ensuring the integrity of transactions, it also means that anyone can potentially track and monitor the financial activity of Ripple and XRP users.

In addition to this, Ripple's technology is also designed to facilitate compliance with anti-money laundering (AML) and know-your-customer (KYC) regulations, which can also raise privacy concerns. In order to comply with these regulations, users are required to provide personal information, including their name, address, and identification documents, which some argue can compromise their privacy.

Another concern around privacy in Ripple and XRP is the potential for third-party access to user data. While Ripple has implemented security measures to protect user data, such as encrypting user data and requiring multi-factor authentication, there is always a risk of third-party access to this data. This could potentially allow hackers or other malicious actors to access sensitive user information, including transaction details and personal data.

Some critics argue that the privacy concerns around Ripple and XRP could hinder adoption of the technology, particularly among users who prioritize privacy and security. Additionally, there are concerns around the potential misuse of user data, including the sale of user data to third-party companies for marketing or other purposes.

Despite these concerns, Ripple has emphasized its commitment to user privacy and security. The company has implemented a number of measures to ensure user privacy, including encryption of user data, multi-factor authentication, and compliance with data protection regulations such as the General Data Protection Regulation (GDPR).

In addition, Ripple has also been working on developing privacy-enhancing features for the Ripple network and XRP. For example, the company has been exploring the use of privacy-preserving technologies such as zero-knowledge proofs and secure multi-party computation to enhance user privacy while still ensuring compliance with regulatory requirements.

Overall, the privacy concerns surrounding Ripple and XRP are a valid criticism of the technology, particularly given the increasing importance of user privacy and security in the digital age. However, Ripple has taken steps to address these concerns and is actively working on developing new privacy-enhancing features for the Ripple network and XRP. As the technology continues to evolve and mature, it is likely that these privacy concerns will become less of an issue, and Ripple and XRP will become even more secure and user-friendly.

The environmental impact of Ripple and XRP

The environmental impact of cryptocurrencies, including Ripple and XRP, has become a growing concern in recent years. While digital currencies offer many benefits, they also require significant amounts of energy to operate. In this section, we will explore the environmental impact of Ripple and XRP and the criticisms the company has faced in this regard.

Energy consumption of Ripple and XRP

Like many cryptocurrencies, Ripple and XRP rely on a decentralized network of computers to validate transactions and maintain the blockchain. This process, known as mining, requires a significant amount of energy consumption, primarily due to the computational power needed to solve complex mathematical algorithms.

However, Ripple and XRP use a different approach to validate transactions, known as consensus validation. Instead of relying on mining, the system uses a group of trusted validators to confirm transactions. This approach is much more energy-efficient than traditional mining methods, as it does not require the same level of computational power.

Despite this, Ripple and XRP still require a significant amount of energy to operate. According to a report by the University of Cambridge, the annual energy consumption of the Ripple network is estimated to be around 5.56 TWh, which is comparable to the energy consumption of the country of Luxembourg.

Criticism of Ripple and XRP's environmental impact

Despite using a more energy-efficient validation method, Ripple and XRP have still faced criticism for their environmental impact. The company has been accused of contributing to climate change and using an unsustainable amount of energy to operate its network.

One of the main criticisms of Ripple and XRP's environmental impact is the carbon footprint associated with energy consumption. The production of energy from fossil fuels, such as coal and natural gas, releases carbon dioxide and other greenhouse gases into the atmosphere, contributing to climate change. As cryptocurrencies become more popular, the energy consumption associated with their operation could lead to significant environmental consequences.

Another criticism of Ripple and XRP is their use of energy from renewable sources. While some cryptocurrency miners have begun to use renewable energy sources, such as solar and wind power, Ripple and XRP have not made a public commitment to using renewable energy. This lack of transparency has led to criticism from environmental activists who argue that the company should take responsibility for its environmental impact and take steps to reduce its carbon footprint.

Efforts to address environmental concerns

Despite facing criticism for their environmental impact, Ripple and XRP have taken steps to address these concerns. In

May 2021, the company announced a plan to achieve carbon net-zero by 2030. The plan includes a commitment to using renewable energy and purchasing carbon offsets to compensate for its carbon emissions.

Ripple has also joined the Crypto Climate Accord, a private-sector-led initiative to decarbonize the cryptocurrency industry. The initiative aims to transition the industry to 100% renewable energy by 2025 and reduce the overall greenhouse gas emissions associated with the operation of cryptocurrencies.

Conclusion

The environmental impact of Ripple and XRP is a growing concern, and the company has faced criticism for its energy consumption and carbon footprint. However, Ripple has taken steps to address these concerns and has committed to achieving carbon net-zero by 2030. While the company's impact on the environment is still significant, it is important to recognize the efforts being made to reduce the environmental consequences of cryptocurrency operations.

Ripple and XRP's response to criticisms

Ripple and XRP have faced various criticisms from the cryptocurrency community, regulators, and environmental advocates. In response to these criticisms, Ripple has taken steps to address these concerns.

Regarding the criticism of centralization, Ripple has acknowledged that the XRP Ledger is currently centralized, but has plans to decentralize the network through its community-driven effort called the XRP Community Fund. The fund aims to support projects and initiatives that advance the decentralization of the XRP Ledger, including the creation of a community-based governance system.

In response to the privacy concerns surrounding XRP, Ripple has highlighted that transactions on the XRP Ledger are public and transparent, similar to Bitcoin and other public blockchains. However, Ripple has also recognized the importance of privacy for certain use cases, and has introduced features such as Payment Channels and the Interledger Protocol to enable private transactions.

Regarding the environmental impact of Ripple and XRP, Ripple has been actively working to reduce its carbon footprint. The company has committed to becoming carbon net-zero by 2030, and has joined the Crypto Climate Accord, a private sector-led initiative to decarbonize the cryptocurrency industry. Ripple has also developed an alternative consensus algorithm called Cobalt, which is designed to reduce energy consumption.

Additionally, Ripple has taken steps to address concerns around the manipulation of the XRP price. The company has implemented measures to prevent insider trading and has pledged to work with regulators to ensure a fair and transparent market.

Furthermore, Ripple has been proactive in engaging with regulators and lawmakers to address concerns around the use of cryptocurrencies for illegal activities such as money laundering and terrorist financing. The company has partnered with leading compliance and regulatory technology providers to ensure that its products and services comply with global regulations.

In conclusion, Ripple has acknowledged and taken steps to address the criticisms it has faced. The company's commitment to addressing concerns around centralization, privacy, the environment, and regulatory compliance demonstrates its commitment to being a responsible participant in the cryptocurrency industry. However, Ripple will need to continue to be responsive to criticisms and take appropriate measures to address them as they arise.

Chapter 9: The Future of Ripple and XRP
The potential for Ripple and XRP to disrupt the financial industry

Ripple and XRP have the potential to disrupt the financial industry in various ways, from reducing transaction costs and settlement times to enabling new use cases and business models. However, their impact on the financial industry will depend on various factors, including regulatory developments, adoption by financial institutions, and competition from other blockchain-based solutions. In this section, we will explore the potential for Ripple and XRP to disrupt the financial industry and transform the way we transact and interact with money.

Reducing Transaction Costs and Settlement Times

One of the key advantages of Ripple and XRP is their ability to reduce transaction costs and settlement times. Unlike traditional payment systems, which rely on intermediaries to facilitate transactions and settle payments, Ripple's technology allows for direct peer-to-peer transfers of value, without the need for intermediaries. This can significantly reduce transaction costs and settlement times, particularly for cross-border payments, which are typically slow and expensive.

For example, in a recent pilot project, Santander Bank used Ripple's technology to enable real-time, low-cost transfers of funds between the United Kingdom and Poland. The project demonstrated that Ripple's technology can reduce the time and cost of cross-border payments, making it an attractive alternative to traditional payment systems.

Enabling New Use Cases and Business Models

Another potential advantage of Ripple and XRP is their ability to enable new use cases and business models. Ripple's technology allows for the creation and exchange of any type of asset, not just traditional currencies. This opens up new possibilities for businesses and individuals to transact and exchange value, including the creation of new digital assets and the tokenization of real-world assets.

For example, Ripple's technology could enable the creation of a new type of digital currency that is backed by a real-world asset, such as gold or real estate. This would provide the benefits of digital currency, such as fast and low-cost transactions, while also providing the stability and security of a real-world asset.

Adoption by Financial Institutions

To realize the full potential of Ripple and XRP, they need to be adopted by financial institutions and integrated into the existing financial infrastructure. Ripple has been making progress in this area, with over 300 financial institutions and payment providers using its technology, including Santander, American Express, and Standard Chartered.

However, adoption by financial institutions is not guaranteed, as many are hesitant to adopt new technology due to concerns around security, compliance, and interoperability with existing systems. Ripple will need to address these concerns and demonstrate the value of its technology to gain wider adoption.

Competition from Other Blockchain-Based Solutions

Finally, Ripple and XRP face competition from other blockchain-based solutions that offer similar advantages, such as low-cost and fast transactions. For example, Stellar, another blockchain-based payment system, has a similar focus on cross-border payments and low transaction costs. Other blockchain-based solutions, such as Ethereum and Cardano, offer more flexibility and programmability, allowing for the creation of more complex smart contracts and decentralized applications.

Ripple and XRP will need to differentiate themselves from these competing solutions and demonstrate their unique value proposition to gain market share.

Conclusion

Ripple and XRP have the potential to disrupt the financial industry and transform the way we transact and interact with money. Their ability to reduce transaction costs and settlement times, enable new use cases and business models, and be adopted by financial institutions are key factors that will determine their impact on the financial industry. However, they also face challenges, including regulatory developments, adoption by financial institutions, and competition from other blockchain-based solutions. The future of Ripple and XRP will depend on how these factors play out and how effectively Ripple can address the challenges ahead.

Future prospects for Ripple and XRP's adoption and growth

As Ripple and XRP continue to evolve, there are several potential factors that could impact their adoption and growth in the future.

Regulation: The outcome of the ongoing SEC lawsuit and any future regulatory developments could have a significant impact on the adoption and growth of Ripple and XRP. If regulatory clarity is achieved and Ripple is able to operate with less uncertainty, it could open up new avenues for adoption and growth.

Partnerships: Ripple's partnerships with financial institutions and payment providers will continue to be a major factor in the adoption and growth of XRP. As Ripple continues to expand its network of partners, it will increase the potential use cases for XRP and drive adoption.

Technology developments: Ripple is constantly working on new developments and improvements to its technology, which could lead to new use cases and increased adoption of XRP. For example, the recent development of the XRPL decentralized exchange (DEX) could provide new opportunities for XRP holders and increase the utility of the token.

Market demand: As more individuals and institutions recognize the benefits of using blockchain technology for payments and remittances, there is potential for increased demand for XRP as a bridge asset. If XRP becomes a widely adopted bridge asset, it could help drive its growth and adoption.

Competition: The cryptocurrency and blockchain space is constantly evolving, and there are numerous competitors to Ripple and XRP in the cross-border payments and remittances space. Ripple will need to continue to innovate and differentiate itself from competitors to maintain its position as a leader in the space.

Economic conditions: Economic conditions can also impact the adoption and growth of XRP. For example, if there is a global economic downturn or recession, it could impact the demand for cross-border payments and remittances, which could in turn impact the adoption and growth of XRP.

Despite these potential factors, the future of Ripple and XRP remains uncertain. However, with a strong network of partners and ongoing developments in technology and regulation, there is potential for Ripple and XRP to continue to disrupt the financial industry and drive adoption and growth in the years to come.

The challenges and opportunities facing Ripple and XRP

Ripple and XRP have made significant strides in the fintech industry and have been recognized for their potential to revolutionize the way financial transactions are conducted. However, like any emerging technology, they face a number of challenges as they strive for widespread adoption and growth.

One of the major challenges facing Ripple and XRP is regulatory uncertainty. As discussed earlier in this book, the SEC lawsuit has cast doubt on the legal status of XRP and the potential implications for Ripple's operations. Additionally, as Ripple seeks to expand its use cases beyond cross-border payments, it may encounter new regulatory hurdles in different jurisdictions.

Another challenge facing Ripple and XRP is the competition from other fintech companies and cryptocurrencies. Although Ripple has established partnerships with major financial institutions, it faces competition from other blockchain-based payment solutions such as Stellar and Bitcoin Cash. Moreover, as the adoption of cryptocurrencies grows, Ripple and XRP may face competition from established players such as Visa and Mastercard, which are also exploring blockchain-based solutions.

Another challenge facing Ripple and XRP is the need to maintain a balance between decentralization and centralization. As discussed earlier, Ripple's critics have raised concerns about the centralization of the XRP ledger and Ripple's control over the network. To address these concerns, Ripple has taken steps to increase decentralization by encouraging the use of validators operated by third parties. However, maintaining this balance will be an ongoing challenge for Ripple and XRP.

Despite these challenges, Ripple and XRP also have a number of opportunities to continue their growth and adoption. One opportunity is the increasing demand for cross-border payments and the potential for Ripple's solutions to reduce the cost and time required for these transactions. Moreover, Ripple's partnerships with major financial institutions give it a strong foothold in the industry and provide opportunities for continued expansion.

Another opportunity for Ripple and XRP is the potential for new use cases beyond cross-border payments. As discussed earlier, Ripple has been exploring new applications for its technology, such as micropayments and supply chain management. If Ripple is successful in expanding its use cases, it could significantly increase the demand for XRP and drive its adoption.

In addition, the increasing interest in cryptocurrency and blockchain technology presents an opportunity for Ripple and XRP to gain wider acceptance and adoption. As more people become familiar with these technologies, they may be more open to using XRP as a means of exchange and a store of value.

Overall, the challenges and opportunities facing Ripple and XRP are complex and interconnected. As Ripple and XRP continue to innovate and expand their solutions, they will need to navigate these challenges while also seizing the opportunities presented by a rapidly evolving fintech landscape. The future of Ripple and XRP remains uncertain, but their potential to disrupt the financial industry cannot be ignored.

The role of Ripple and XRP in shaping the future of money

As the world becomes increasingly digital and global, the role of cryptocurrencies like Ripple and XRP in shaping the future of money is becoming more important. While there are still many challenges facing the adoption and growth of these technologies, there are also many opportunities for Ripple and XRP to play a key role in the evolution of money.

One potential role for Ripple and XRP in shaping the future of money is in the area of cross-border payments. As we have seen, the current system for cross-border payments is slow, expensive, and often unreliable. Cryptocurrencies like XRP have the potential to revolutionize this system by offering fast, low-cost, and secure transactions across borders. This could have a profound impact on the way that money moves around the world and could help to increase economic activity and reduce poverty in developing countries.

Another area where Ripple and XRP could play a significant role is in the development of new financial products and services. As we have seen, the technology behind Ripple and XRP is incredibly versatile and can be used for a wide range of applications. This means that there are many opportunities for developers and entrepreneurs to create innovative new financial products and services using Ripple and XRP. This could include everything from peer-to-peer lending platforms to automated investment advisors to decentralized exchanges.

In addition to these applications, Ripple and XRP also have the potential to play a key role in the emerging field of decentralized finance (DeFi). DeFi is a new financial system that operates on top of blockchain technology and is designed to be more open, transparent, and accessible than traditional finance. Ripple and XRP could be used to power a wide range of DeFi applications, including stablecoins, decentralized exchanges, and lending platforms.

Of course, there are also many challenges that Ripple and XRP will need to overcome in order to play a significant role in shaping the future of money. One of the biggest challenges is regulatory uncertainty. As we have seen, cryptocurrencies are still a relatively new and untested technology, and there is still a great deal of uncertainty surrounding how they will be regulated in the future. This could make it difficult for Ripple and XRP to gain widespread adoption and could limit their potential impact on the financial industry.

Another challenge is competition from other cryptocurrencies and blockchain platforms. While Ripple and XRP have many unique features and advantages, there are also many other cryptocurrencies and blockchain platforms that are vying for a place in the financial system. This means that Ripple and XRP will need to continue to innovate and improve their technology in order to stay competitive and to attract new users.

Despite these challenges, the potential for Ripple and XRP to shape the future of money is enormous. By offering fast, secure, and low-cost transactions across borders, enabling the development of innovative new financial products and services, and powering the emerging field of decentralized finance, Ripple and XRP have the potential to transform the financial industry and to create a more open, transparent, and accessible financial system for everyone.

Conclusion and final thoughts on the future of Ripple and XRP

Ripple and XRP have already achieved a significant amount of success in the financial industry. They have demonstrated the potential to revolutionize cross-border payments and have gained adoption from various financial institutions. Despite facing criticisms and regulatory challenges, Ripple has continued to innovate and expand its ecosystem.

The potential for Ripple and XRP to disrupt the financial industry goes beyond just cross-border payments. They have the potential to transform the entire financial system by providing faster, cheaper, and more efficient payments and settlements. Ripple's technology can also facilitate the creation of new financial products and services that were previously not possible.

As the use cases for Ripple and XRP continue to grow, so does the potential for their adoption and growth. The financial industry is becoming more open to new technologies, and Ripple is well-positioned to take advantage of this shift. The company has already gained the trust of many financial institutions, and its partnerships with major players in the industry are only expected to grow.

However, Ripple and XRP still face challenges, including regulatory hurdles and concerns over centralization and environmental impact. The company will need to continue to work closely with regulators to ensure compliance with laws and regulations. It will also need to address concerns over centralization and environmental impact to maintain its credibility and reputation in the industry.

Despite these challenges, Ripple and XRP have a bright future ahead. They have already made significant strides in revolutionizing cross-border payments, and their potential to transform the financial industry is only just beginning to be realized. As more financial institutions adopt Ripple's technology, the ecosystem will continue to grow and evolve, creating new opportunities for innovation and growth.

In conclusion, the future of Ripple and XRP looks promising. While there are challenges and obstacles to overcome, the potential benefits are significant. Ripple and XRP have already proven their ability to innovate and disrupt the financial industry, and they are well-positioned to continue to do so in the years to come. As the financial industry continues to evolve and embrace new technologies, Ripple and XRP will likely play a significant role in shaping the future of money.

Conclusion

Recap of the main points covered in the book

In this book, we have explored the potential of Ripple and XRP as a game-changing technology in the world of finance. We have delved into the history of Ripple and XRP, examined the technology behind the system, and discussed its use cases and potential impact on the financial industry. In this final chapter, we will recap the main points covered in the book.

Firstly, we discussed the history of Ripple and XRP, including the background of the founders and the development of the technology. We also explored the differences between Ripple and XRP, and how they work together to facilitate cross-border payments.

Secondly, we explored the technology behind Ripple and XRP. We discussed the consensus algorithm used by the Ripple network, the role of validators, and the benefits of using a decentralized network for cross-border payments.

Thirdly, we looked at the potential use cases of Ripple and XRP beyond cross-border payments. We discussed how the technology could be used in areas such as micropayments, remittances, and even identity verification.

Fourthly, we examined the potential impact of Ripple and XRP on the financial industry. We discussed how the technology could disrupt traditional payment systems and the potential benefits for consumers, banks, and other financial institutions.

Fifthly, we explored the criticisms of Ripple and XRP, including concerns around centralization, privacy, and environmental impact. We also discussed how Ripple and XRP have responded to these criticisms.

Sixthly, we discussed the future prospects for Ripple and XRP's adoption and growth. We looked at the challenges and opportunities facing the technology, and how they could affect its future success.

Finally, we examined the role of Ripple and XRP in shaping the future of money. We discussed how the technology could revolutionize the financial industry and what it could mean for the future of global commerce.

Overall, this book has highlighted the potential of Ripple and XRP as a disruptive technology in the world of finance. While there are still challenges to overcome, the potential benefits of the technology are enormous. As we look towards the future, it is clear that Ripple and XRP will continue to play an important role in shaping the future of money.

Reflection on the significance of Ripple and XRP in the financial industry

In conclusion, Ripple and XRP have the potential to revolutionize the financial industry by providing a fast, secure, and cost-effective means of cross-border payments. Throughout this book, we have explored the technology behind Ripple and XRP, their use cases, their potential impact on the financial industry, and their criticisms.

Reflecting on the significance of Ripple and XRP in the financial industry, it is clear that they have the potential to be a game-changer. Currently, cross-border payments can take several days to complete, and the process is often cumbersome, involving several intermediaries, resulting in high costs for both the sender and receiver. Ripple and XRP offer a solution that can significantly reduce transaction times and costs, making cross-border payments accessible to people who may have previously been excluded from the financial system.

Furthermore, Ripple and XRP's potential goes beyond cross-border payments. They can be used for various financial applications, including trade finance, micropayments, and peer-to-peer transactions. As more businesses and individuals recognize the benefits of Ripple and XRP, we can expect to see their adoption continue to grow.

However, Ripple and XRP are not without their criticisms. Concerns about centralization, privacy, and environmental impact have been raised. These criticisms must be addressed for Ripple and XRP to realize their full potential.

Despite these criticisms, Ripple and XRP have shown a commitment to compliance and regulatory compliance, and have been proactive in addressing these concerns. As the financial industry continues to evolve, it is essential to consider the role Ripple and XRP may play in shaping its future.

In conclusion, Ripple and XRP offer a promising solution to some of the challenges facing the financial industry today. While they are not without their challenges, the potential benefits they offer cannot be overlooked. As they continue to develop and mature, Ripple and XRP are likely to play an increasingly important role in the financial industry, bringing the world closer together by facilitating fast, secure, and cost-effective cross-border payments.

Final thoughts on the potential of Ripple and XRP to transform the financial landscape

In conclusion, Ripple and its digital asset XRP have the potential to revolutionize the financial industry in numerous ways. Throughout this book, we have explored the history, technology, use cases, potential impact, criticisms, and future prospects of Ripple and XRP.

One of the main takeaways from this book is that Ripple and XRP have the potential to significantly improve cross-border payments. The current system is slow, expensive, and fraught with inefficiencies. By using blockchain technology and a digital asset, Ripple and XRP can enable near-instant and low-cost cross-border payments that benefit both individuals and institutions.

Moreover, Ripple and XRP have the potential to disrupt other industries beyond payments. For example, they can be used for supply chain management, remittances, micropayments, and more. Ripple's partnerships with various institutions, including banks and payment providers, indicate that there is significant interest in its technology.

Despite the potential benefits, Ripple and XRP face several challenges. One of the most significant criticisms of Ripple is its centralization, as the company controls a large portion of the XRP supply. Additionally, there are concerns about privacy and environmental impact.

However, Ripple and XRP have been proactive in addressing these criticisms. For example, Ripple has committed to making its operations carbon-neutral by 2030, and it has been working on decentralizing the XRP ledger. The company has also been working on integrating privacy features into its technology.

Looking to the future, Ripple and XRP have the potential to transform the financial landscape in significant ways. The growth of blockchain technology and digital assets is likely to continue, and Ripple is well-positioned to be a major player in this space.

As we move forward, it will be essential to continue monitoring Ripple and XRP's progress and evolution. It is likely that there will be many twists and turns along the way, and the potential impact of Ripple and XRP on the financial industry remains to be seen. However, it is clear that Ripple and XRP are here to stay and have the potential to change the way we think about money and finance.

In conclusion, Ripple and XRP represent a fascinating case study of how blockchain technology and digital assets can be leveraged to improve financial systems. The potential benefits are significant, but so are the challenges. It will be interesting to see how Ripple and XRP navigate these challenges and continue to grow and evolve in the years to come.

THE END

Glossary

Below, you'll find a comprehensive list of important vocabulary and their corresponding definitions regarding Ripple and XRP.

Ripple: A San Francisco-based technology company that develops and operates a global payment network called RippleNet.

RippleNet: A decentralized network of banks and financial institutions that use Ripple's technology to facilitate cross-border payments and settle transactions in real-time.

XRP: A digital asset that serves as the native currency of the RippleNet payment network. XRP is used to facilitate transactions and as a bridge currency between different fiat currencies.

Distributed Ledger Technology (DLT): A digital system that records and stores data in a decentralized and secure manner, allowing for the creation of tamper-proof and transparent digital records.

Consensus Protocol: A mechanism by which participants in a distributed network agree on the validity of a transaction or data entry, and confirm its inclusion in the ledger.

Interledger Protocol (ILP): A protocol developed by Ripple that enables different ledgers to communicate and exchange value with each other, facilitating cross-border payments between different payment networks.

Smart Contracts: Self-executing digital contracts that automatically enforce the terms and conditions of a contract, without the need for intermediaries or third parties.

Centralized: A system or organization where control and decision-making authority is concentrated in the hands of a single entity or group of entities.

Decentralized: A system or organization where control and decision-making authority is distributed among all participants in the network, with no single entity having full control.

Digital Asset: A digital representation of a physical or intangible asset, such as a currency, commodity, or stock. XRP is an example of a digital asset.

Cryptocurrency: A type of digital asset that uses cryptography to secure and verify transactions and control the creation of new units. XRP is a cryptocurrency.

Blockchain: A type of DLT that uses cryptographic techniques to create a secure and tamper-proof ledger of transactions. XRP uses a unique type of blockchain known as the XRP Ledger.

Potential References

Introduction:

"Ripple" Wikipedia,
https://en.wikipedia.org/wiki/Ripple_(payment_protocol)

"XRP" Ripple, https://ripple.com/xrp/

"What is Ripple?" Investopedia,
https://www.investopedia.com/terms/r/ripple-cryptocurrency.asp

Chapter 1: The Birth of Ripple and XRP

"The History of Ripple" CoinCentral,
https://coincentral.com/history-ripple/

"The Origins of Ripple Labs and the Birth of XRP" Medium,
https://medium.com/coinmonks/the-origins-of-ripple-labs-and-the-birth-of-xrp-5c5b258b06c8

"What is Ripple? The story behind the banking revolution nobody is talking about" Wired,
https://www.wired.co.uk/article/ripple-explained

Chapter 2: The Advantages of XRP

"XRP vs Bitcoin: What's the Difference?" CoinCentral,
https://coincentral.com/xrp-vs-bitcoin/

"Why XRP Will Succeed and Why It Might Not" Forbes,
https://www.forbes.com/sites/forbestechcouncil/2018/06/25/why-xrp-will-succeed-and-why-it-might-not/?sh=10b50ef064b7

"What is XRP? The ultimate guide to Ripple and XRP" Decrypt, https://decrypt.co/resources/what-is-xrp-the-ultimate-guide-to-ripple-and-xrp

Chapter 3: The Adoption of Ripple and XRP

"Why Ripple's XRP is getting more traction with banks than bitcoin" CNBC, https://www.cnbc.com/2018/02/27/why-ripples-xrp-is-getting-more-traction-with-banks-than-bitcoin.html

"How Ripple is Winning over Banks and Influencing the Future of Blockchain" The Verge, https://www.theverge.com/2018/4/4/17185052/ripple-blockchain-bitcoin-coinbase-startup-silicon-valley

"SWIFT to Introduce Blockchain via GPI Link, Rival Ripple in Cross-border Payments" Forbes, https://www.forbes.com/sites/michaeldelcastillo/2020/12/15/swift-to-introduce-blockchain-via-gpi-link-rival-ripple-in-cross-border-payments/?sh=5a9d22c11a5a

Chapter 4: Ripple and XRP in the Cryptocurrency Market

"The Ultimate Guide to Ripple and XRP" Blockonomi, https://blockonomi.com/ripple-xrp-guide/

"Ripple (XRP) Price Analysis: Is The Value Of XRP Above The Trend Line Or In The Triangle?" ZyCrypto, https://zycrypto.com/ripple-xrp-price-analysis-is-the-value-of-xrp-above-the-trend-line-or-in-the-triangle/

"Why XRP's Rise Is Different Than Bitcoin's" Investopedia, https://www.investopedia.com/news/why-xrps-rise-different-bitcoins/

Chapter 5: The Ripple Community

"Ripple for Good Announces $25 Million Donation to Expand Financial Inclusion Worldwide." Ripple. Accessed September 20, 2021. https://ripple.com/insights/ripple-for-good-announces-25-million-donation-to-expand-financial-inclusion-worldwide/.

"Ripple Developer Center." Ripple. Accessed September 20, 2021. https://developers.ripple.com/.

"Ripple Developer Portal." GitHub. Accessed September 20, 2021. https://github.com/ripple.

"Ripple Donates $29 Million to Support Public Schools in the US." Ripple. Accessed September 20, 2021. https://ripple.com/insights/ripple-donates-29-million-to-support-public-schools-in-the-us/.

"Ripple Launches $50 Million Blockchain Research Initiative." Ripple. Accessed September 20, 2021. https://ripple.com/insights/ripple-launches-50-million-blockchain-research-initiative/.

"Ripple Offers $100 Million in Funding for Game-Changing Blockchain Projects." Ripple. Accessed September 20, 2021. https://ripple.com/insights/ripple-offers-100-million-in-funding-for-game-changing-blockchain-projects/.

"Ripple's Xpring Launches Platform to Build Decentralized XRP Projects." CoinDesk. Accessed September 20, 2021. https://www.coindesk.com/ripples-xpring-launches-platform-to-build-decentralized-xrp-projects.

"XRP Ledger Dev Portal." GitHub. Accessed September 20, 2021. https://github.com/XRPLF.

"XRPChat Forum." XRPChat. Accessed September 20, 2021. https://www.xrpchat.com/.

"Xpring Developer Center." Xpring. Accessed September 20, 2021. https://developer.xpring.io/.

Chapter 6: The Regulation of Ripple and XRP:

"The U.S. Regulatory Framework for Cryptocurrencies" by Andrea Tinianow and Robert Cohen (2018)

"Ripple and XRP: A Regulatory Overview" by Stephanie Bodoni (2020)

"Crypto Asset Regulation: A Comparative Analysis" by Dirk A. Zetzsche, Ross P. Buckley, Douglas W. Arner, and Janos Nathan Barberis (2019)

"What happens to XRP if Ripple wins case against the SEC?" Finbold News January 5, 2023. https://finbold.com/what-happens-to-xrp-if-ripple-wins-case-against-the-sec/.

"SEC Charges Ripple and Two Executives with Conducting $1.3 Billion Unregistered Securities Offering" US Securities and Exchange Commission, FOR IMMEDIATE RELEASE 2020-338. https://www.sec.gov/news/press-release/2020-338.

"Ripple CEO Discusses Potential Outcomes of SEC Lawsuit Over XRP" Bitcoin.com July 27, 2022. https://news.bitcoin.com/ripple-ceo-discusses-potential-outcomes-of-sec-lawsuit-over-xrp/.

Chapter 7: The Potential of Ripple and XRP:

"The Future of Money: How Digital Currencies Will Change the World" by J. Gerard Feehan (2020)

"The Fintech Revolution: The Ripple Effect" by Tom Glocer (2018)

"The Fourth Industrial Revolution" by Klaus Schwab (2017)

Chapter 8: The Criticisms of Ripple and XRP:

"Ripple Effect: The Cryptocurrency Craze Continues" by Benjamin Biard and Kunal M. Parker (2019)

"The Dark Side of Cryptocurrencies: Illicit Activities, Money Laundering, and Terrorism Financing" by Tal Berman and Arun Sharma (2019)

"Why Ripple Isn't Ready for Prime Time" by Matthew De Silva (2018)

Chapter 9: The Future of Ripple and XRP:

"The Future of Money: How Digital Currencies Will Change the World" by J. Gerard Feehan (2020)

"The Future of Fintech and Banking: Digitally disrupted or reimagined?" by Penny Crosman (2020)

"The Internet of Money" by Andreas M. Antonopoulos (2014)

Conclusion:

"Blockchain Basics: A Non-Technical Introduction in 25 Steps" by Daniel Drescher (2017)

"The Future Is Faster Than You Think: How Converging Technologies Are Transforming Business, Industries, and Our Lives" by Peter H. Diamandis and Steven Kotler (2020)

"The Blockchain and the New Architecture of Trust" by Kevin Werbach (2018)

www.ingramcontent.com/pod-product-compliance
Lightning Source LLC
Chambersburg PA
CBHW072208060526
44654CB00047B/1468